J

from the

Masters

⌘ ⌘ ⌘

Messages

from the

Masters

A Cosmic Book
of
Galactic Wisdom

Ted Mahr

Foreword by Hon. Paul Hellyer

ISBN-13: 978-1976391446
ISBN-10: 197639144X

Limits of Liability and Disclaimer of Warranty
The author and publisher shall not be liable for your misuse of this material. This book is strictly for informational and educational purposes.

Warning – Disclaimer
The purpose of this book is to educate and entertain. The author and/ or publisher do not guarantee that anyone following these techniques, suggestions, tips, ideas, or strategies will become successful. The author and/or publisher shall have neither liability nor responsibility to anyone with respect to any loss or damage caused, or alleged to be caused, directly or indirectly by the information contained in this book.

Cover Design: Carolyn White
Interior Design: Carolyn White
Editor: Gerry White
Except as noted, water crystal Images in Chapter Nine Copyright 2017 Office Masaru Emoto. LLC.

Contents

Foreword

This book, which may be considered a bit "far out" by some readers, is as fascinating as it is important. Theodore Mahr has used his psychic gifts to take us on an incredible journey into the realm of life after death so we can learn from ancient masters and powerful politicians speaking with the benefit of hindsight.

For me it has been most helpful to have a number of so-called conspiracy theories substantiated by fact. President Kennedy lists the diverse co-conspirators who plotted and executed his murder. He also paints a beautiful picture of what the world might have been like had he survived.

President Eisenhower confirms that he met with both good, and self-seeking aliens including the Reptilians who first blackmailed and then betrayed him. A representative of the Galactic Federation, Valiant Thor, actually lived in the Pentagon from 1957 to 1960. He offered us a world of peace and well-being, including the elimination of sickness. He was rejected by power-mongers like Richard Nixon, who had friends in the pharmaceutical industry, and by the Chiefs of Staff, who refused to give up the nuclear technology "that has been banned by all enlightened civilizations throughout the universe as it can only lead to death and destruction."

The most re-assururing words came from Nostradamus and Leonardo da Vinci who indicate that the woeful predictions of an apocalyptic armageddon no longer apply, and that the future of humanity is very bright if we strive for ascension to a higher dimension, and accept the fact that the universe is a unity, and the glue that holds it together is love. All we have to do is seek to love and serve the God who created a universe of love and light.

Hon. Paul Hellyer, Former Minister of Defense for Canada

Preface

I was asked by the great spirits to write this book – great spirits including Professor Albert Einstein, J. Robert Oppenheimer, Michele de Nostradamus, Leonardo da Vinci, U.S. President John F. Kennedy, Senator Robert F. Kennedy, Dr. Masaru Emoto, Mahatma Gandhi, Nicolai Tesla, U.S. President Dwight D. Eisenhower, and the Galactic Alliance – so their cosmic messages of Galactic Wisdom can help bring humanity and the planet from darkness into light. And they all tell me that the time is now for this information to be released.

They say that we are all souls inhabiting a physical body. We inhabit bodies to learn lessons in this Earth school, in order to ascend. We are all like students in different classes – some are young or new souls, just learning their soul lessons. Others are very old souls who have come back here to the planet to help humanity ascend. I have been here for approximately 52,000 years, or 720 lifetimes, with the sole purpose of raising consciousness, so humanity and the planet may ascend. All of my great spirit friends on the other side sincerely hope that you will read and listen to their very profound and important messages!

Earth is slated for ascension into the higher dimensions. As of September 2016, the planet shifted into positive energy for the first time in at least 26,000 years. For thousands of years, the Schumann resonance or the vibration of the planet was at 7.83 Hz. Then on January 31, 2017, for the first time in recorded history, the Schumann resonance reached frequencies of 36+ Hz.[1]

As of May 8th, 2017, the frequency of the planet has now spiked to up to 120 Hertz.[2]

---

1   http://www.drjoedispenza.com/blog/consciousness/what-does-the-spike-in-the-schumann-resonance-mean/
2   http://whispersfromthesoul.com/2017/05/schumann-resonance-spikes-may-8th-110-120-hertz/

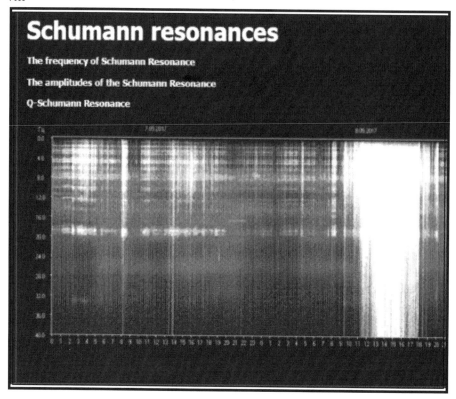

Image Source: http://whispersfromthesoul.com/schumann-resonance-spikes-may-8th-110-120-hertz/

I am sure it will be even higher in the future, as we shift into the 5th Dimension!

More positive shifts are coming, but the good news is that as a result of this shift, there will be no World War III and no Armageddon. We will of course have many challenges, including environmental problems like Fukushima and the secret world wide chem-trail program. However, by working together, we can and will turn this planet around.

We are all powerful spiritual beings destined to evolve into the higher dimensions. With the help of the Supreme Being (or Prime Creator), we are destined to create a beautiful, bright future not only for ourselves, but for our children, and many future generations. The true nature of humanity on Earth is to be kind, loving, and benevolent. If we make the right choices (and I know we will), we can and will create a much happier and harmonious planet – an Earth free of all conflict and war, where we can all live as one. We all have the spark of the Supreme Being, the prime creator, or God within all of us. In that sense, we are all one – regardless of our creed, race, or culture. Once we realize we are all one, the wars, negativity, and conflict currently on the planet will disappear.

This ascension process could have happened over 50 years ago if U.S. President John F. Kennedy's life had not been cut short on November 22, 1963. Had he lived, the United States would now be exchanging ambassadors with other benevolent human and extraterrestrial civilizations. Our longevity would have easily doubled to over 150 years. The Federal Reserve would have been abolished decades ago. Money would be deemphasized as a medium of exchange, because there would be free energy. The entire planet would live in peace and harmony – we would be far more materially and spiritually richer than we are today, as war would have become a thing of the past.

Now through the 2020s will be pivotal decades in the spiritual evolution of humanity; we are at a crossroads! We can take the high road and continue our spiritual development. Or we can go down the negative path of conflict and war. However, I know that there is a bright, beautiful future ahead of all of us on this planet – and I know we will make the right choices to transform this planet into a beautiful and wonderful place — not just for ourselves but our children and children's children!

I hope your will enjoy this book, and the messages from these great men of history. These messages are meant as a guide book for humanity to create a beautiful, happy, and loving planet!

⌘ ⌘ ⌘

Acknowledgments

This book could not have been written without the help of my wonderful father, Col. Raymond A. Mahr. He brought me into this world and helped raise me to be who I am today. I also want to thank my wonderful foster mother Teri, who taught me how to communicate with the other side, and to work for a better and happier planet! I also thank my wonderful, loving, and kind spirit friends on the other side – Professor Albert Einstein, J. Robert Oppenheimer, Nostradamus, Leodardo da Vinci, U.S. President John F. Kennedy, Senator Robert F. Kennedy, Dr. Masaru Emoto, Mahatma Gandhi, Nicolai Tesla, U.S. President Dwight D. Eisenhower, Zorra of the Hollow Earth, and the Galactic Alliance – for all their messages and for asking me to write this book.

In addition, I want to thank my dear friends for all her support and encouragement, including (a) Michiko Hayashi, the Global Director of the Emoto Peace Project, and everyone in her wonderful office in Tokyo, Japan, (b) Scott Lemriel, who put me in contact with the Galactic Alliance, (c) Paul Hellyer who wrote a wonderful foreward to the book, and (d) my dear friends Carolyn and Gerry White of Olympia who provided encouragement, graphic design and proof read the manuscript. I also thank Erika, for providing me with a wonderful place to write this book and many, many other light workers. I could not have written this book without all of their help!

This work is meant to be a beacon of hope in a world that is sometimes filled with doom and gloom. I hope this will bring much needed light and love, and sunshine to the world – let there be light!

⌘ ⌘ ⌘

Introduction

I am a psychic. I grew up in a psychic family, and have been in touch with the other side since 1994, or over 23 years. Thus, it is just as easy for me to talk to the other side and to spirits and people who have passed on, as it is for me to talk with people in this dimension.

My journey to make the Earth a better and happier planet actually started 720 lifetimes, or 52,000 years ago when I came here from Arcturus, via the Pleiades Constellation. According to my friend Simon Parkes, I came down from the 6th Dimension from a life in Arcturus to the 5th Dimension of the Pleiades, to learn how to be human, so I could come to Earth and help raise the consciousness and vibration of this planet. Thus, I have been here on Earth for a long time.

I was here during Atlantean times 12,500 years ago when a group of power hungry, negative people ended up destroying both Atlantis and Lemuria in a nuclear war. As a priest in one of the temples in Atlantis, my friends and I tried to turn things around, but we failed and Atlantis destroyed itself. Many of the same entities who were present during these Atlantean times have come back today — some have learned their lesson and have come back to help this planet become a beautiful, harmonious place. Others have not learned their lesson and are trying to destroy this beautiful planet. Fortunately, this time, the positive light forces will succeed — I know we will raise consciousness and make this a better and happier place! Both Professor Einstein and Nikola Tesla were in Atlantis 12,500 years ago—they also tried to stop that civilization from destroying themselves. They and all of their great spirit friends want their messages and this book to be an inspiring blue book for creating a beautiful, new planet Earth. If we can all work together, I know we will succeed!

⌘ ⌘ ⌘

Professor Albert Einstein

Contact with the Great Spirits

Tuning into the other side requires concentration and lots of positive, high energy. Love and good thoughts are the currency of the other side.

My first contact with the great spirits came over two years ago during one beautiful spring day in March 2014, when I was walking through this beautiful forest. The sun light was streaming through the trees in many sunbeams. I had just spent most of the day working on scripting my radio show -- I have a metaphysical radio show called "Out of this World Radio," which broadcasts out of Seattle and Bellevue, Washington in the United States on Fridays from 2 pm to 4 pm PST at www.outofthisworld1150.com.

I was in a positive, high energy mood. I had been meditating on what a great man Professor Einstein was -- and while I was walking through this forest, he suddenly came to me, and started communicating with me telepathically. When speaking to spirits like Professor Einstein on the other side, it is important to realize that there are twelve different dimensions. The twelfth Dimension is God or the Supreme Being. Although we exist in the Third Dimension, Professor Einstein and the great spirits I speak with typically exist in the fifth and higher dimensions. There is physicality in the fifth Dimension where Professor Einstein exists, and this dimension is just as real as this third Dimension – it is just different.

As my friends on the other side tell me, there is no such thing as "death." When you pass over, you usually make a transition to the fifth dimension, a higher and lighter existence. Because time exists only in the fourth Dimension, there is no time in the fifth Dimension. Thus, there is no past, present, or future in the fifth Dimension – everything just "exists in the now." This is why a good psychic can go into the fifth Dimension, and see into the past, present, or future with great accuracy. This is also why a good psychic can do what is called "remote viewing" and see through time (see: Appendix A on "Contacting the Spirit World and Proof of the Other Side")

Messages from Professor Einstein

One of the first messages the Professor gave me was planet Earth was slated for ascension into the 5th and higher dimensions. As humanity spiritually evolves, the veil between these higher dimensions will become less and less, to the point where the entire planet would shift into the fourth and quickly into the fifth Dimension. Professor Einstein likes to be called Professor Einstein or Albert; he does not like to be called just "Einstein" – he feels it is disrespectful.

Professor Einstein and the other great spirits have many other enlightening and profound messages for humanity, especially now as the planet was rapidly evolving into the higher dimensions. He said that there was no reason why he and his friends could not talk to humanity from the other side now – he and his friends want to not only continue the work that they did here when they were in the third Dimension on planet Earth, but also to help us evolve spiritually. They want us to help us create the beautiful planet that we are supposed to create!

This is a time of truth – things which are true will become truer. Falsehoods will be seen for what they are and simply fall by the wayside. This would apply to governments, corporations, and individuals in their private lives.

The Professor emphasized "we are all one." This was among his most important messages, one he wrote about during his life on Earth. When he was alive, he wrote: "As human beings we are part of the whole yet we experience our thoughts and feelings as something separated from the rest of creation – a kind of optical delusion of consciousness. This becomes a kind of prison, restricting us to our personal desires and affection for a few persons nearest to us. Our task must be to free ourselves from this prison by widening our circle of compassion to embrace all living creatures and the whole of Nature in its beauty."[1]

At the time of our first conversation in February 2015, he told me the planet was getting ready to shift into what he termed the "positive." Although the majority of the people at that time were still negative, soon the entire planet would shift into this positive energy. As it happened, the shift occurred in September 2016. Although we still do of course face many challenges, our future is very bright. There will be no World War III, nor any other nuclear holocaust.

When I asked Professor Einstein about the atomic bomb, he immediately told me he was used as a "pawn" when he wrote a letter to President Roosevelt to develop the atomic bomb in 1939. He learned from the other side that nuclear technology is actually illegal on all other inhabited planets in this Milky Way Galaxy since it can only be used as a destructive force. Humans on this planet did not actually develop the atomic bomb. The information used came from a group of extra-terrestrials known as the Reptilians and the Greys (a cloned robotic slave species). They actually gave us the technology so that we would destroy ourselves. Professor Einstein says that Nazi scientists during the 1930s were not any smarter than other scientists elsewhere in the world. However, the difference is that they did have a lot of help from the Greys and the Reptilians which feed off negative emotions created by war and destruction.

⌘   ⌘   ⌘

1   http://www.goodreads.com/quotes/369-a-human-being-is-a-part-of-the-whole-called

We are all souls or light beings inhabiting a physical body in the Third Dimension. All of us have the spark of the creator or the Supreme Being within us. We have the ability to communicate with spirits in the higher dimensions. As a psychic, I regularly go into the fifth and higher dimensions to communicate with spirits, angels, and those who have passed on. So when Professor Einstein came to me, I was very happy. He had much to tell me. My first conversation with Professor Einstein lasted about two hours, and he gave me many amazing messages. It was the first of many amazing and life changing conversations with him.

The Bomb of Love

Professor Einstein told me if he could do this life over, he would never work on the atomic bomb – he would have preferred to work in a restaurant or remain a patent clerk in Switzerland, than participate in a technology that could easily destroy the planet. Nuclear technology is far too destructive. He said nothing good can come of it. He only realized later, instead of creating a bomb of destruction, he should have created a "bomb of love," as explained in this letter.[1]

In this beautiful letter, Professor Einstein writes,

"When I proposed the theory of relativity, very few understood me, and what I will reveal now to transmit to mankind will also collide with the misunderstanding and prejudice in the world. I ask you to guard the letters as long as necessary, years, decades, until society is advanced enough to accept what I will explain below.

There is an extremely powerful force that, so far, science has not found a formal explanation to. It is a force that includes

---

[1]   https://suedreamwalker.wordpress.com/2015/04/15/a-letter-from-albert-einstein-to-his-daughter-about-the-universal-force-which-is-love/

and governs all others, and is even behind any phenomenon operating in the universe and has not yet been identified by us.

This universal force is LOVE.

When scientists looked for a unified theory of the universe they forgot the most powerful unseen force.

Love is Light that enlightens those who give and receive it. Love is gravity, because it makes some people feel attracted to others. Love is power, because it multiplies the best we have, and allows humanity not to be extinguished in their blind selfishness. Love unfolds and reveals.

For love we live and die. Love is God and God is Love. This force explains everything and gives meaning to life. This is the variable that we have ignored for too long, maybe because we are afraid of love because it is the only energy in the universe that man has not learned to drive at will.

To give visibility to love, I made a simple substitution in my most famous equation.

If instead of $E = mc2$, we accept that the energy to heal the world can be obtained through love multiplied by the speed of light squared, we arrive at the conclusion that love is the most powerful force there is, because it has no limits.

After the failure of humanity in the use and control of the other forces of the universe that have turned against us, it is urgent that we nourish ourselves with another kind of energy

If we want our species to survive, if we are to find meaning in life, if we want to save the world and every sentient being that inhabits it, love is the one and only answer.

Perhaps we are not yet ready to make a bomb of love, a device powerful enough to entirely destroy the hate, selfishness and greed that devastate the planet.

However, each individual carries within them a small but powerful generator of love whose energy is waiting to be released.

When we learn to give and receive this universal energy, we will have affirmed that love conquers all, is able to transcend everything and anything, because love is the quintessence of life.

I deeply regret not having been able to express what is in my heart, which has quietly beaten for you all my life. Maybe it's too late to apologize, but as time is relative, I need to tell you that I love you and thanks to you I have reached the ultimate answer."
~ Albert Einstein

Professor Einstein considers love to be the most powerful force in the universe. Love can be used to transform this world into the beautiful, harmonious planet, home for the magnificent humans we are destined to become.

He also told me that he had been a scientist during Atlantis when it too was destroyed in a nuclear war approximately 12,500 years ago. He and I both lived and knew each other during Atlantean times, and we had both tried to stop the "madness" during those days, but was unsuccessful. However, this time we will be successful in turning this planet around! He said the Earth and humanity will be transformed into a beautiful and harmonious place!

Albert told me that both of our souls were linked together as part of the same soul family before he reincarnated at end of the 19th century into a family in Switzerland. Our hair styles and even the way we look resemble each other. He went to Switzerland for his scientific life mission to raise consciousness and I went to the United States. He contacted me because our souls are linked. He said it is time for these messages to be given to humanity.

In this regard he is now working on a spiritual telephone that will enable the ascended masters and other friends (see below) the ability to talk directly to anyone here on Earth in the Third Dimension. He is looking for spiritually minded scientists and engineers to work with him on this side of the veil, so together we can make this a reality in the next five to ten years. If there are any scientists or engineers who would like to help with this spirit phone, please contact me.

⌘   ⌘   ⌘

Leonardo da Vinci

Contact with the Great Spirits

Image Source: https://en.wikipedia.org/wiki/Leonardo_da_Vinci

During my first conversation with Professor Einstein, he asked if I would like to meet his friends. I replied that his friends were also my friends. Thus, I would love to meet them! So the first person that Professor Einstein introduced me to was Leonardo da Vinci, the famous 16th century Italian inventor.

Leonardo da Vinci is a fascinating man who was many centuries ahead of his time. Leonardo told me he actually learned to astral travel and remote view many things in the far future. His drawings of flight machines and other fantastic objects came from his ability to time travel. For example, machines like submarines came from his astral travel into the 20th Century.

He can also see into our future. He says, "the destiny of humanity and planet Earth is indeed very bright! Free energy will be available to everyone within a very short time — the stranglehold the oil companies have had on our world economy will cease to exist within the next 5 to 10 years," depending what choices people make during this critical time in human history.

Leonardo is still very much with us today, and he works with Professor Einstein on shared projects, including the spiritual phone. He says this new special phone will allow communication with the other side of the veil as easily as making a telephone call!

⌘   ⌘   ⌘

J. Robert Oppenheimer

Contact with the Great Spirits

1904 - 1967

After Leonardo da Vinci, the second great spirit Professor Einstein introduced me to was J. Robert Oppenheimer. Mr. Oppenheimer is a very kind soul, who deeply cared about humanity's future. During World War II, he helped create the Atomic Bomb in the United States.

When he first saw the Trinity atomic bomb explode in the desert of New Mexico on July 16, 1945, Professor Oppenheimer said, "We knew the world would not be the same — a few people laughed — a few people cried — most people were silent. I remember the line from the Hindu scripture, the Bhagavad Gita— Vishu is trying to persuade the prince that he should do his duty, and to impress him, takes on his multi-armed form, and says, Now I have become death, the destroyer of worlds — I suppose we all thought that — one way or another..."[1]

Dr. Oppenheimer immediately went into a deep depression and regretted his participation in the development and use of the atomic bomb, as did Professor Einstein. Professor Oppenheimer feels as Professor Einstein does that he was used as a pawn. He now works with Professor Einstein, Leonardo da Vinci, and other great spirits on the other side to help us create a more beautiful and peaceful world.

Nuclear technology has been banned by all enlightened civilizations throughout the universe as it can only lead to death and destruction. All three great spirits (Professor Einstein, Mr. Oppenheimer, and Mr. Da Vinci) say that there is free energy already available on this planet the oil companies and others have hidden. The good news is it is only a matter of time before these free energy technologies become available to all humanity.

---

[1]   https://en.wikipedia.org/wiki/J._Robert_Oppenheimer and https://www.youtube.com/watch?v=dus_M4sn0_I

Nikola Tesla

Contact with the Great Spirits

Image Source: https://en.wikipedia.org/wiki/Nikola_Tesla

After talking to these great spirits, Professor Einstein introduced me to another friend of his, Nikola Tesla. In my opinion, Mr. Tesla was one of the greatest inventors of the 19th and 20th centuries.

He led the way in producing free energy – his dream was to provide free energy for the entire planet before he passed away in January, 1943. Unfortunately, before he could realize this dream, he tells me he was stopped by the greed of some people who wanted to make people pay for all of their energy needs.

Mr. Tesla also says that he was actually murdered. When he died, the U.S. Government took all of his discoveries and information on free energy. He says that they did not release it to the public, but instead used it later in their secret space program. Both Professor Einstein and Mr. Tesla and I were living in Atlantis at the same time I was there 12,500 years ago when a small negative group of people destroyed the planet in a nuclear war. He says we all worked to try and change the course of history back then, but we failed.

However, because planet Earth is destined to ascend, he said we are all back again trying to raise consciousness. What is amazing is that he said many of the negative entities here today, including George Bush Sr. and Jr., and Dick Cheney, were present during the Atlantean times. They helped destroy the Earth back then. Mr. Tesla said they had not learned their lesson – they are back again now to try and destroy the planet. However, this time, he said that the light forces will win – and the planet will ascend!

in 1899, Nikola Tesla had a fascinating interview with a journalist named John Smith, in which Mr. Tesla said, "Everything is light." He said he "... wanted to illuminate the whole earth. There is enough electricity to become a second sun. Light would appear around the equator, as a ring around Saturn. I am part of a light, and it is the music. The Light fills

Newton learned that the secret is in geometric arrangement and motion of celestial bodies. He recognized that the supreme law of harmony exists in the Universe. The curved space is chaos, chaos is not music. Einstein is the messenger of the time of sound and fury."[1] Mr. Tesla believed that we are all one. And as we ascend into the higher dimensions, he said we will realize that we are in fact all part of a really beautiful Universe.

⌘   ⌘   ⌘

---

1   http://sciencevibe.com/2017/04/05/teslas-sad-last-interview-im-a-defeated-man-i-wanted-to-illuminate-the-whole-earth/

⌘   ⌘   ⌘

Senator Robert F. Kennedy

Contact with the Great Spirits

Picture of Senator Kennedy just before he was shot from behind at the Ambassador Hotel in Los Angeles in 1968.[1]

---

[1] https://www.buzzfeed.com/briangalindo/17-haunting-images-that-capture-rfks-assassination?utm_term=.wfRVdYXwar#.jmnkl934Mn

Shortly after I spoke with Mr. Oppenheimer and Mr. Tesla, Professor Einstein introduced me to Senator Robert F. (Bobby) Kennedy. I was so happy because I greatly admired and respected both him and his brother, President John F. Kennedy. Bobby Kennedy said Sirhan Sirhan did not kill him – the real killer was a CIA paid assassin named Thane Eugene Cesar. Robert Kennedy was killed with a bullet fired into his neck at very close range; Cesar stood behind RFK while Sirhan Sirhan stood in front. Cesar was a security guard assigned to protect JFK in the Ambassador Hotel.

Bobby Kennedy told me the CIA had actually planned his murder. They knew he would have reopened the investigation into his brother's assassination once elected President. The CIA clearly did not want that to happen, since that agency had helped plan the murder of JFK. The CIA agent (Thane Eugene Cesar) who murdered RFK fled to the Philippines the day after the murder. Cesar (who is still alive) has resided there ever since with a nice U.S. Government pension, as a reward for his "services". Below is a photograph of Cesar taken in 1968[1]:

Thane Eugene Caesar, security guard

---

[1]   https://riversong.wordpress.com/rfk-the-other-kennedy-assassination

Bobby also said that Sirhan Sirhan was actually a mind controlled MK Ultra CIA robot. Bobby said he was brainwashed by another CIA agent, a lady in a white polka-dot dress who was also on the scene. She whispered a code-word into Sirhan's ears which triggered him to start shooting. Ironically none of the bullets fired by Sirhan Sirhan even struck the Senator. The real evidence pointing to the murder was completely buried by the police in Los Angeles, under pressure from the CIA.

A recent book, *Coup D'état in America: The CIA and the Assassination of John F. Kennedy*, also confirms that the bullet that actually killed Bobby Kennedy was fired at very close range (within an inch or so) behind RFK's head – the only person in that position was Thane Eugene Cesar – NOT Sirhan Sirhan. According to an interview with the authors of the Coup D'état book, RFK's autopsy "...was performed by Dr. Thomas Noguchi, then the chief medical examiner-coroner of Los Angeles County." When asked about his conclusions, the author said, "Noguchi's exemplary autopsy showed that the fatal shot was fired at close range on an upward angle from behind Kennedy, entering below his right ear" (emphasis supplied). Explaining what he meant by close range, Noguchi said, "When I say 'very close,' we are talking about the term of either contact or a half inch to one inch in distance." Sirhan was always in front of Kennedy, at a distance variously estimated at between one and six feet. Noguchi's autopsy also showed that Kennedy was hit two other times from behind – and a fourth shot fired from behind went through his suit coat without hitting him. Noguchi was later run out of office for his unorthodoxy." [1]

Researchers from the Mary Farrell Foundation state Sirhan has no memory of the events at the time RFK was killed at the Ambassador Hotel in Los Angeles. Accordingly, this "has led many to believe that he may have been a real 'Manchurian

---

[1]   Interview at: http://www.thesleuthjournal.com/rfk-interview/.

Candidate,' programmed to shoot RFK and then fail to recall who put him up to it." Accordingly, Sirhan was seen in the hotel — including in the pantry itself — in the company of a girl wearing a polka-dotted dress. The girl and another male companion were seen running from the pantry after the shooting. RFK campaign worker Sandy Serrano, taking a break out on a balcony, saw them run from the hotel, the woman gleefully shouting, "We shot him. We shot him." When Serrano asked who they meant, the girl replied "Senator Kennedy." In fact, they write that, "unbelievable as this sounds, their behavior was corroborated by LAPD officer Paul Sharaga, who was told the same thing by an elderly couple in the parking lot behind the hotel. Sharaga was the source of an All-Points Bulletin (APB) on the suspects. The girl was described consistently by most of the witnesses: dirty blond hair, well-built, with a crooked or 'funny' nose, wearing a white dress with blue or black polka-dots." They also write that "there were many other witnesses to the polka-dotted dress girl, in the hotel and in the company of Sirhan in the weeks prior to the assassination."[2]

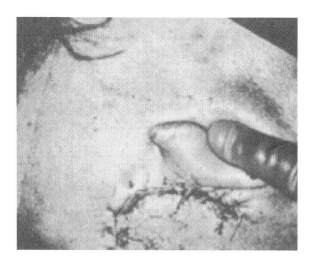

Autopsy photo of RFK and bullet hole entry into rear of neck.[3]

[2]   https://www.maryferrell.org/pages/Robert_Kennedy_Assassination.html
[3]   http://www.thesleuthjournal.com/rfk-interview/

The authors of the book, *Coup D'Etat in America: The CIA and the Assassination of John F. Kennedy*, state "it was not certain RFK would win the nomination, and he was trailing Hubert Humphrey even after the California victory, but RFK's California win and momentum made it seem likely that he could get the nomination. Humphrey was tarnished by being Lyndon Johnson's vice president and by supporting the Vietnam War, unlike RFK at that time. So RFK's California victory was the tipping point that caused him to be killed. Eugene McCarthy was not a particularly strong candidate, despite having beaten RFK in Oregon, the first time a Kennedy had lost an election. RFK probably would have gone on to receive the nomination and to win the general election. The war would have been ended. His brother had been starting to deescalate the war when he was killed in 1963. The military-industrial complex needed to get rid of both Kennedys to continue the war. Noam Chomsky's book on JFK and the war is hostile to JFK but makes the intriguing point that although it's generally believed the war was lost by the United States, those who backed it 'won' in a sense because they made so much money from it. They didn't care about the Americans who were killed, let alone the millions of Vietnamese and Cambodians."[1]

Once Bobby Kennedy passed over to the other side, he had full access to universal consciousness – he could ask any question he wanted and instantly be given the truth. For example, when he asked about who killed his brother (President John F. Kennedy), he learned the real killers of his brother, including:

(a) the CIA, who was furious that JFK had not invaded Cuba;

(b) George Bush Sr., who Bobby said came from a family of "Nazis and Nazi sympathizers" – he said Bush was actively involved with the CIA and helped plan his murder;

---

[1]   http://www.thesleuthjournal.com/rfk-interview/.

(c) Vice President Lyndon Baines Johnson, who wanted JFK dead so he could become the President of the U.S. without waiting for another 4 or 5 years. LBJ was also under investigation for murder in Texas and was about to be arrested and indicted when JFK was murdered. Once LBJ became U.S. President, he could not be tried for any crimes under the U.S. Constitution and LBJ knew it;

(d) All the banks of the Federal Reserve, who were furious that JFK had started issuing "U.S. Notes" from the U.S. Treasury, thereby bypassing their banks. The Federal Reserve, a private banking system, has been issuing money illegally since 1913 when it was created. Only the U.S. Treasury can legally issue U.S. currency under Article 7 of the U.S. Constitution. Bobby says our currency system in the United States is fraudulent and illegal. On June 4, 1963, JFK signed Executive Order 11110, "with the authority to basically strip the Federal Reserve Bank of its power to loan money to the United States Federal Government at interest. With the stroke of a pen, President Kennedy declared that the privately owned Federal Reserve Bank would soon be out of business."[2]

The number "1111" is considered an Angelic number. The so called "Federal Reserve" not "Federal" nor "Reserve". It is privately owned by the following banks, organized for profit as a commercial enterprise:

- Rothschild Bank of London
- Rothschild Bank of Berlin
- Lazard Brothers of Paris
- Israel Moses Seif Banks of Italy
- Warburg Bank of Amsterdam
- Warburg Bank of Hamburg
- Lehman Brothers of New York
- Kuhn Loeb Bank of New York

[2]   http://www.rense.com/general76/jfkvs.htm

- Goldman, Sachs of New York
- Chase Manhattan Bank of New York [3]

Bobby says that all of these banks worked jointly with the CIA and the Mafia to murder his brother. He quotes Mayer Amschel Rothschild, who said "Let us control the money of a nation, and we care not who makes its laws." [4]

(e) Israel, who wanted JFK dead because President Kennedy had asked Israel to stop making an atomic bomb. David Ben-Gurion (Prime Minister of Israel, November 1955 - June 1963) first ordered the assassination of JFK, in collaboration with the CIA and Mafia, among others. The order was followed up by Levi Eshkol (Prime Minister of Israel from June 1963 to 1969). Israel felt President Kennedy had no business stopping them from acquiring an atomic bomb; they were prepared to do anything to stop JFK, including activity participating and collaborating in his murder;

(f) The Mafia, who were furious about losing their casinos and investments in Cuba. They blamed JFK for not invading that country so that they could get their investments back. The Mafia also were very angry with Bobby Kennedy for what they said was his "double cross." The Mafia had helped elect JFK. However, Bobby as Attorney General under the Kennedy Administration had prosecuted organized crime across the country. The Mafia felt he had unfairly turned against them.

Bobby said that there were three shooters who killed his brother: (1) one was from the French Mafia who shot JFK from the "grassy knoll," (2) one was from the Italian Mafia who also shot JFK, and (3) another shooter who fired from underneath a street drainage manhole cover.

3   http://www.federalbudget.com/fed.html
4   https://history.stackexchange.com/questions/7887/did-rothschild-say-this-famous-quote-if-yes-what-did-he-mean-by-it See also: G. Edward Griffin, The Creature from Jekyll Island: A Second Look at the Federal Reserve (May 1998);

St. John Hunt's father (who was CIA) was also involved."[5]
Bobby said that both Mafia shooters were quickly whisked
out of the U.S. after the assassination. They returned to
their homes in France and Italy, where they lived for many
years before passing away of natural causes in the 1990s.

Bobby explained that one of the reasons why the CIA was (and is) so
ruthless, is that they were actually started with thousands of Nazis
and SS men after World War II, under the leadership of Allen Dulles.
Dulles himself was a Nazi sympathizer and loved Adolf Hitler.[6]

After speaking with Bobby Kennedy, I asked him if he could please
put me in contact with his brother, President John F. Kennedy,
which he did. When I asked Bobby Kennedy if I could speak to his
brother, John F. Kennedy, he replied, "sure, would you like to talk to
him now? He's right here." I said I would be honored, and he came
right in. Since then, I have been in constant contact with President
Kennedy. JFK is one of the many reasons why I wrote this book.

President Kennedy likes to be called either "Jack" or "Professor
Kennedy" now. He says his role now is to help raise human
consciousness, and to educate people about the coming beautiful
new Earth. He feels the title "President" brings up negative images
of his murder. Jack is now trying to teach humanity to raise
their vibrations, so both the people and the planet can ascend.

⌘   ⌘   ⌘

---

[5]   St. John Hunt, Bond of Secrecy: My Life with CIA Spy and Watergate Conspirator
E. Howard Hunt (2012).
[6]   "Allen Dulles, the Nazis, and the CIA", http://www.panshin.com/trogholm/secret/
rightroots/dulles.html

President John F. Kennedy

Messages from President John F. Kennedy on our bright, beautiful future

According to President Kennedy, "The forces which cut my life short on November 22, 1963 still control the United States and the world, but their power is declining — there is a very bright and happy future for humanity! It is our destiny as the people of this planet to become a loving, benevolent society living in harmony. The time has come for all of us to create the bright, beautiful future that I know we all want!"

He then wanted me to add his famous inauguration speech of January 21st, 1961: "... And so my fellow Americans, ask not what your country can do for you, ask what you can do for your country ... My fellow citizens of the world, ask not what America will do for you, but what together we can do for the freedom of man." These words are even more important today — Jack would only change his words to: "My fellow citizens of the world, ask not what America will do for you, but what together we can do for the freedom of all peoples to create a beautiful and peaceful planet."

Jack tells me we had a chance to make this wonderful transformation into the higher dimensions when he was President in the early 1960s. At that time, he attempted to: (1) abolish the Federal Reserve, (2) rein in the Central Intelligence Agency, and (3) approach the Soviet Union to establish a joint space program with genuine collaboration instead of conflict and competition. The same cycles which were present in the 1950s and early 1960s have come back, except that the changes for a better and happier planet are coming from the bottom up — not the top down (as in JFK's time).

Jack says it is our destiny to become a much better and happier people who live in true peace and harmony. The entire planet is shifting rapidly into the higher dimensions. Jack said his murder was an "inside job," by an alliance between Lyndon Baines Johnson, J. Edgar Hoover, George Bush Sr., the CIA, the private banks of the Federal Reserve, and the Mafia, as his brother Bobby learned when he passed over to the other side.

Jack says Lee Harvey Oswald was in fact a "patsy" who was set up. The news of his assassination was leaked by the U.S. Embassy in Auckland New Zealand by mistake one day early. They released the prepared story of Oswald murdering Jack Kennedy before the actual murder occurred! The U.S. Embassy in Auckland was part of the cover up to blame Oswald for the murder. He said the Embassy was ordered by what Jack calls the "secret government" to present this contrived press release of his assassination by Oswald on November 22nd, 1963. However, they forgot that Auckland is one day ahead of the United States, so they mistakenly released the news about his assassination in New Zealand on November 22nd, a day early.

Image from http://christchurchcitylibraries.com/Heritage/ Newspapers/Star23Nov1963/output/page_01.asp

Because Auckland is 18 or 19 hours head of the U.S. west coast, the Embassy in Auckland released news about JFK's assassination when it was actually November 21st in the United States (or one day before JFK was actually murdered). Communications were not as fast in the 1960s with no internet. They were able to cover up the misinformation in the confusion that resulted after his murder. Also people trusted government much more in those days than now. They were not as prone to question everything as they do today. Below is a link to the front page of the Christchurch Star, New Zealand newspaper, in which the news of JFK's assassination was released early.

According to the Christchurch Star, "There were claims that The Christchurch Star coverage contained information which was pre-packaged by conspirators prior to the assassination taking place, and distributed in the United States and then sent out to New Zealand very soon after the event. They say Oswald's background was reported far too quickly and it must have been a CIA-planted cover story."

An episode in the film JFK also features 'Mr X', identified by Oliver Stone later as Air Force Colonel L. Fletcher Prouty (1917 - 2001). Prouty served in the Pentagon and was shown being sent out of the way to Antarctica by those who had planned the assassination. Played by actor Donald Sutherland, Mr X is seen buying a copy of The Christchurch Star on the morning of 23 November 1963 at Christchurch Airport."[1]

President Lyndon Baines Johnson (LBJ) was also actively involved, because Jack says that Johnson did not want to wait until 1968

---

[1]   http://my.christchurchcitylibraries.com/the-christchurch-star-23-november-1963/#ChristchurchStar

to run for President. Jack says that Johnson had murdered other people before and his criminal activities were catching up to him. The FBI was ready to indict him for criminal activities in Texas in November 1963, when he helped to murder Jack Kennedy.

Under the U.S. Constitution, Jack confirmed that Johnson knew he could avoid prosecution for any crimes while he was a sitting president. Johnson knew in his twisted, sick mind that he had to kill President Kennedy. Jack says that the same people at the CIA (including George Bush Senior) who helped murder Jack were also responsible for killing his brother Senator Robert F. Kennedy. This is because if elected, RFK was going to fully investigate Jack's murder.

⌘ ⌘ ⌘

Professor Kennedy Explains about the New Earth

Jack Kennedy tells me that our planet has been slated for ascension into the higher spiritual realms for quite some time. If the right choices had been made in 1963, and the assassination had been thwarted, we would live in a very different world today.

For example, the Federal Reserve would have been deemed unconstitutional and abolished by now. No private bank including the Federal Reserve has any legal authority to issue US currency. JFK calls the entire set up of the Federal Reserve a complete "legal sham." The Federal Reserve has been operating in open violation of the U.S. Constitution since its inception in 1913. This is a direct quote from Jack Kennedy.

There was another U.S. President who stood up to the big private banks: Abraham Lincoln. Jack also says he was murdered by the same private banking interests which murdered Jack. He tells me there was no such thing as a "lone gunman" like Oswald. From his perspective on the other side, there is only truth. As a spirit, Jack now has access to what he calls "universal truth."

He clearly sees the truth of what happened during his assassination. Allen Dulles was the leader of the co-conspirators who planned and executed his murder. Ironically, LBJ appointed Dulles to the Warren Commission to supposedly help uncover Jack's real murderers. Jack says this is like assigning the "fox to guard the hen house."

Jack states if you are going to murder someone and you want to cover it up, do it in a city like Dallas or Los Angeles. This is because the police departments "have been completely corrupt for decades." Thus, it was very easy to cover the murder of his brother, Senator Robert F. Kennedy, who was murdered in 1968 in Los Angeles.

In my opinion, Jack Kennedy was one of the greatest Presidents the United States has ever had. Jack did what he thought was right for the country. Unlike many of our current politicians, he told the truth, and was sincere. And I think he actually was the last freely elected President of the United States.

Jack knew what he was up against when he make his "Secret Societies Speech." He wants me to give you some passages from that narrative which are still relevant today.

This transcript is part of this Secret Societies Speech that Jack Kennedy gave at on April 27, 1961 before the American Newspaper Publishers Association:

"The very word 'secrecy' is repugnant in a free and open society; and we are as a people inherently and historically opposed to secret societies, to secret oaths and secret proceedings. We decided long ago that the dangers of excessive and unwarranted concealment of pertinent facts far outweighed the dangers which are cited to justify it. Even today, there is little value in opposing the threat of a closed society by imitating its arbitrary restrictions. Even today, there is little value in insuring the survival of our nation if our traditions do not survive with it. And there is very grave danger that an announced need for increased security will be seized upon those anxious to expand its meaning to the very limits of official censorship and concealment. That I do not intend to permit to the extent that it is in my control. And no official of my Administration, whether his rank is high or low, civilian or military, should interpret my words here tonight as an excuse to censor the news, to stifle dissent, to cover up our mistakes or to withhold from the press and the public the facts they deserve to know.

For we are opposed around the world by a monolithic and ruthless conspiracy that relies on covert means for expanding its sphere of influence--on infiltration instead of invasion, on subversion instead of elections, on intimidation instead of free choice, on guerrillas by night instead of armies by day. It is a system which has conscripted vast human and material resources into the building of a tightly knit, highly efficient machine that combines military, diplomatic, intelligence, economic, scientific and political operations.

Its preparations are concealed, not published. Its mistakes are buried not headlined. Its dissenters are silenced, not praised. No expenditure is questioned, no rumor is printed, no secret is revealed.

No President should fear public scrutiny of his program. For from that scrutiny comes understanding; and from that understanding comes support or opposition. And both are necessary. I am not asking your newspapers to support the Administration, but I am asking your help in the tremendous task of informing and alerting the American people. For I have complete confidence in the response and dedication of our citizens whenever they are fully informed.

I not only could not stifle controversy among your readers—I welcome it. This Administration intends to be candid about its errors; for as a wise man once said: 'An error does not become a mistake until you refuse to correct it.' We intend to accept full responsibility for our errors; and we expect you to point them out when we miss them.

Without debate, without criticism, no Administration and no country can succeed — and no republic can survive. That is why the Athenian lawmaker Solon decreed it a crime for any citizen to shrink from controversy. And that is why our press was protected by the First (emphasized) Amendment — the only business in America specifically protected by the Constitution— not primarily to amuse and entertain, not to emphasize the trivial and sentimental, not to simply 'give the public what it *wants' — but to inform, to arouse, to reflect, to state our dangers and our opportunities, to indicate our crises and our choices, to lead, mold educate and sometimes even anger public opinion.*

This means greater coverage and analysis of international news — for it is no longer far away and foreign but close at hand and local. It means greater attention to improved understanding of the news as well as improved transmission. And it means, finally, that government at all levels, must meet its obligation to provide you with the fullest possible information outside the narrowest limits of national security...

And so it is to the printing press — to the recorder of mans deeds, the keeper of his conscience, the courier of his news — that we look for strength and assistance, confident that with your help man will be what he was born to be: free and independent."[1]

Jack says that there was a Coup d'Etat here in the United States in 1963. The Coup d'Etat changed Presidential leadership from a freely elected one (JFK) to an unelected President (LBJ). As a result, the country has had problems ever since. This is because the U.S. has been controlled by a very secretive and negative cabal. The "... monolithic and ruthless conspiracy ..." that threatened the world in 1961 is still very much alive today. Many dissenters are "silenced, not praised." No expenditure is questioned, no rumor is printed and no secret is revealed.

However, Jack wants to emphasize that "Without debate, without criticism, no Administration and no country can succeed — and no republic can survive. That is why the Athenian lawmaker Solon decreed it a crime for any citizen to shrink from controversy." Jack says people in the coming new Earth will be what they were born to be: "free and independent."

[1]   http://www.thepowerhour.com/news3/jfk_speech:_transcript.htm)

Jack says that his words are as important today as they were 56 years ago in 1961 when he made this profound speech. The "... very word 'secrecy' is repugnant in a free and open society; and we are as a people inherently and historically opposed to secret societies, to secret oaths and secret proceedings." Unfortunately in today's America, only six corporations own and control over 90 percent of the mass media. As Lord Acton said in 1887, "Power tends to corrupt, and absolute power tends to corrupt absolutely[2]." With this concentration of power over the mass media in the United States, Jack says that the media is "completely corrupted."

I then asked Jack to speak with President Eisenhower, and he replied, "yes, of course!" He put me right in touch with Ike.

⌘　⌘　⌘

---

[2]   http://www.phrases.org.uk/meanings/absolute-power-corrupts-absolutely.html

President Eisenhower

Contact with the Great Spirits

From: www.whitehouse.gov/1600/presidents/dwightdeisenhower

U.S. President Dwight D. Eisenhower (aka "Ike") was an honorable man, He wanted to do the right thing for both America and the world. When he was elected President on November 4, 1952, the U.S. had just come out of the Second World War. The U.S. and the world faced many challenges. In 1953, within months after he was first elected, he met with a group of benevolent, advanced humans from the Pleiades Constellation. The Pleiadians offered the U.S. spiritual and technological help, but they wanted us to get rid of all of our nuclear weapons. Although he liked the Pleiadians, he turned down their offer because: (1) the United States was in a cold war at the time with the Soviets, and (2) he felt that the U.S. needed the weapons.

Within six months after meeting with the Pleiadians, the Reptilians and the Greys contacted President Eisenhower. They met with him in March 1954 at Edwards Air Force Base in southern California while he told the press that he was going to a "dental appointment."

When the Reptilian/Grey UFO landed at the end of the runway at Edwards A.F.B., President Eisenhower met with the Reptilian Ambassador. The Reptilian ET offered President Eisenhower some of their advanced technology to fight the Soviet Union. In exchange, the Reptilians wanted the "right" for them and their subservient slave species (the robotic Greys) to "abduct" and "study" humans. As part of this proposal, the Reptilians agreed to give the U.S. Government a list of those abducted. The Reptilians also assured President Eisenhower that the people who were abducted would be returned "unharmed."

Unlike the Pleiadians, President Eisenhower did not like the Reptilians and Greys. When he first refused their offer, the Ambassador told Eisenhower that if he did not sign the agreement, they would offer their technology to the Soviets. The Soviets would then become the preeminent power on Earth. Reluctantly, President Eisenhower agreed to the deal, and our history has never been the same since.

Ike says during the meeting, the Reptilians used mind control devices on him so he would sign the agreement. Only later did President Eisenhower find out that the Reptilians were negotiating the same exact agreement with the Soviets, which the Soviets also agreed to. Of course, the agreement was completely illegal, as it was never ratified by the U.S. Congress — and the public never knew about it.

President Eisenhower tells me that this agreement was definitely the worst decision of his life. He has regretted it ever since. He said that he should have realized that eventually relations between the two countries would eventually improve. Eventually, there would no longer be any cold war between the two countries. Thus, there would be no need for the agreement.

Jack Kennedy says that President Eisenhower told him about the agreement. President Eisenhower says that the agreement was called the "Treaty of Grenada.[1]" The treaty was entered into with the Reptilians and Greys which allowed the aliens to abduct humans, in exchange for some of their advanced technology to fight the Soviets.

President Eisenhower had called it the worse decision of his entire life — and Ike warned JFK the White House had been completely cut off from any kind of role in the secret alien/U.S. military bases in Nevada. This technology was being transferred to the U.S. Military in these secret bases. However, President Eisenhower explained that he had no control over the bases, and what was worse, parts of the bases were not under human control!

For example, in 1959, when President Eisenhower tried send a

---

[1]   See: Dr. Michael Salla, "Eisenhower's 1954 Meeting with Extraterrestrials" at: https://www.bibliotecapleyades.net/exopolitica/esp_exopolitics_Q_0.htm

representative from his office to S-4 and Area 51 in Nevada to try and find out what was going on, his representative was refused. Only after he threatened to send the Sixth Army Group out of Denver did the CIA, U.S. Military, and Reptilians running the secret bases in Nevada allow President Eisenhower's representative to enter.

However, President Eisenhower now wants the world to know about this decision because he wants it to end! America and the world have suffered enough. All the negativity and constant warfare have been encouraged and engineered by the Reptilians and their slave species. President Eisenhower, Jack Kennedy, and Bobby Kennedy all say it is time for humanity as a whole to get rid of these negative creatures, and their influence!

⌘   ⌘   ⌘

Valiant Thor

In spite of this 1954 agreement with the Reptilians, President Eisenhower tells me that he also had a second chance to gain wonderful and positive spiritual and technological help — this was with a positive ET entity named Valiant Thor three years later in 1957.

In that year, Valiant Thor, another representative of the Galactic Alliance, offered President Eisenhower spiritual and technological assistance, as well as help in getting rid of the Reptilians and the Greys. This time, President Eisenhower tells me that he was in favor of the agreement — however, President Nixon and the Joint Chiefs of Staff were all against it, because Mr. Thor offered no weapons.

Valiant had also offered free energy and the elimination of all diseases from the planet. However, Nixon in particular was against this — he had many friends in the pharmaceutical industry and U.S. medical establishment. Nixon was afraid that they would all lose their jobs, if all disease was eliminated from the planet.

In 2013, Hollywood Film Director Craig Compobasso produced a wonderful film called *Stranger at the Pentagon*.[1] The film documented the visit of Valiant Thor to the White House in 1957. Valiant was actually given accommodations at the Pentagon to live for three years (from 1957 to 1960), until JFK was elected.

The follow page shows a picture of Mr. Thor, on the left, taken in the late 1950s:

---

[1]   http://www.imdb.com/title/tt2645374/

Image Source: http://www.ufosightingsdaily.com/2012/02/president-
eisenhower-had-three-secret.html

⌘   ⌘   ⌘

President Eisenhower's Speech on the Military—Industrial Complex

This agreement with the Reptilians and the Greys led to President Eisenhower's famous speech where he warned about the dangers of the U.S. Military – Industrial complex in 1959. The key part of his speech is where he said, "Yet, in holding scientific research and discovery in respect, as we should, we must also be alert to the equal and opposite danger that public policy could itself become the captive of a scientific technological elite." The relevant parts of his important and very profound speech are as follows, in which he warned us of the dangers of the military-industrial complex. He wanted me to include the full speech here:

"We now stand ten years past the midpoint of a century that has witnessed four major wars among great nations. Three of these involved our own country. Despite these holocausts America is today the strongest, the most influential and most productive nation in the world. Understandably proud of this pre-eminence, we yet realize that America's leadership and prestige depend, not merely upon our unmatched material progress, riches and military strength, but on how we use our power in the interests of world peace and human betterment.

Throughout America's adventure in free government, our basic purposes have been to keep the peace; to foster progress in human achievement, and to enhance liberty, dignity and integrity among peoples and among nations. To strive for less would be unworthy of a free and religious people. Any failure traceable to arrogance, or our lack of comprehension or readiness to sacrifice would inflict upon us grievous hurt both at home and abroad.

Progress toward these noble goals is persistently threatened by the conflict now engulfing the world. It commands our whole attention, absorbs our very beings. We face a hostile ideology—global in scope, atheistic in character, ruthless in purpose, and insidious in method. Unhappily the danger it poses promises to be of indefinite duration. To meet it successfully, there is called for, not so much the emotional and transitory sacrifices of crisis, but rather those which enable us to carry forward steadily, surely, and without complaint the burdens of a prolonged and complex struggle—with liberty the stake. Only thus shall we remain, despite every provocation, on our charted course toward permanent peace and human betterment ....

The record of many long years stands as proof that our people and their government have, in the main, understood these truths and have responded to them well, in the face of threat and stress. But threats, new in kind or degree, constantly arise. Of these, I mention two only.

A vital element in keeping the peace is our military establishment. Our arms must be mighty, ready for instant action, so that no potential aggressor may be tempted to risk his own destruction. Our military organization today bears little resemblance to that known by any of my predecessors in peacetime, or indeed by the fighting men of World War II or Korea.

Until the latest of our world conflicts, the United States had no armaments industry. American makers of plowshares could, with time and as required, make swords as well. But now we can no longer risk emergency improvisation of national defense; we have been compelled to create a permanent armaments industry of vast proportions. Added to this, three and a half million men and women are directly engaged in the defense establishment. We annually spend on military security alone more than the net income of all United States corporations.

Now, this conjunction of an immense military establishment and a large arms industry is new in the American experience. The total influence—economic, political, even spiritual—is felt in every city, every State house, every office of the Federal government. We recognize the imperative need for this development. Yet we must not fail to comprehend its grave implications. Our toil, resources and livelihood are all involved; so is the very structure of our society.

In the councils of government, we must guard against the acquisition of unwarranted influence, whether sought or unsought, by the military-industrial complex. The potential for the disastrous rise of misplaced power exists and will persist. We must never let the weight of this combination endanger our liberties or democratic processes. We should take nothing for granted. Only an alert and knowledgeable citizenry can compel the proper meshing of the huge industrial and military machinery of defense with our peaceful methods and goals, so that security and liberty may prosper together ...."[1]

Both Jack Kennedy and President Eisenhower say this is the reason why they have been giving me the messages for this book. They say the American people and the world need to know they are still very much alive on the other side – they are want humanity to awaken!

As President Eisenhower outlines now, "We should take nothing for granted. Only an alert and knowledgeable citizenry can compel the proper meshing of the huge industrial and military machinery of defense with our peaceful methods and goals, so that security and liberty may prosper together." Once published and widely disseminated, both JFK and President Eisenhower say that their messages (and the messages of the other great spirits in this book), will help make the American people (and the world) more alert and knowledgeable. This will allow Earth to now ascend into the higher dimensions — and we can together create

---

1   http://whowhatwhy.org/2016/01/17/he-told-us-so-president-eisenhowers-military-industrial-complex-speech/):

a bright, beautiful future for ourselves and future generations!

For example, when President Eisenhower made this famous speech against the Military Industrial Complex in 1959, he was actually talking about how he had lost control of segments of his government and the military after he had signed this 1954 secret agreement. In fact, when he was refused access to the military base in Nevada, he realized that he had lost control over his own government. Since 1959, no White House representative has been allowed into Area 51. The last time any U.S. President tried to gain entry to the base was President John F. Kennedy — this was on November 12, 1963 when he issued an Executive Order to the CIA to disclose all UFO files. The CIA refused to comply with this request, and 10 days later, President Kennedy was murdered.[2]

Since the 1950s, the Reptilians and Greys have abducted approximately 6 million humans. They have returned only about 1.5 million of those people — the rest have been killed, eaten, or taken into slavery by the Reptilians and the Greys. For those who can remember, many children were abducted by the Greys and the Reptilians especially during the 1970s and 1980s.

For some Americans growing up during these years, the pictures of lost and missing children on milk cartons are directly related to these abductions. For many millions of children, they were never returned. During this time, the Greys in particular would like to kill and then drain the blood of terrified children, in which they would then swim in a pool of their blood. The U.S. Government did not stop the Greys and Reptilians from

2   In Larry Holcombe's book, *The Presidents and UFOs: A Secret History from FDR to Obama.* he cites a classified CIA communication from 1961 that reads, in part, "when conditions become nonconductive for growth in our environment and Washington cannot be influenced any further . . . it should be 'wet.'". 'Wet' was the Soviet code for "assassination," and Holcombe believes this could be the CIA code for a plot to kill Kennedy. See: http://exopolitics.org/tag/kennedy-assassination/   See also: Dr. Michael Salla's excellent book, *Kennedy's Last Stand: Eisenhower, UFOs, MJ-12 & JFK's Assassination* and http://exopolitics.org/kennedys-last-stand-roots-of-jfk-assassination-lie-in-what-he-saw-in-1945/

this practice. It has only been stopped recently, thanks to a policing action by the Galactic Alliance. The Galactic Alliance is an alliance of 450 million planets in this one third part of the Milky Way Galaxy where our planet (Earth) is located. They are comprised of about 7 trillion entities, and they are mostly (but not all) human; however, they are all benevolent.

I have been in contact with U.S. President Eisenhower on the other side for the past three years. He tells me that his decision to sign this agreement with the Reptilians and the Greys has allowed a nonhuman species to take control of not only the United States, but also the world.

Both President Eisenhower and Jack Kennedy say that many U.S. companies are now largely controlled by the Greys and Reptilians, especially Monsanto, which specializes in genetic engineering. The Reptilians consider themselves the "master geneticists" of the universe. President Eisenhower tells me they have shared their technology with Monsanto. Another company is Geico, a large American insurance company they both tell me is controlled by the Reptilians. As one example, for years Geico has used bipedal walking alligators who like to eat humans in their insurance ads as per the following commercial screen shot:[3]

3   www.ispot.tv/ad/A1vW/geico-alligator-arms-its-what-you-do

Other Geico commercials portray "geckos" (lizard like creatures) as being warm, friendly creatures, with jet black eyes. The problem with the geckos used in their commercials is that these lizard like creatures have large black eyes as evidenced by the picture below of gecko in Geico commercial:[1]

These "geckos" in the commercials look very much like the Greys, which are a slave species of the Reptilians as seen in this picture.[2] Note the eyes of a typical Grey.

1   www.facebook.com/thegeicogecko/photos/a.444927416483.247066.193023956483/
10152286836456484/?type=1&theater
2   http://alien-ufo-research.com/the-greys/

The problem is that real geckos on this planet have cat like eyes as seen in these photos below.

For generations of Americans (and especially children) who have been watching these Geico "gecko" (Grey ET) commercials, when the Greys present themselves to the American people, President Eisenhower says that they will be accepted as warm, friendly creatures — just as they have

been depicted in the Geico commercials for many years. Other people in many public and private institutions are controlled by the Reptilians and the Greys through implants.

⌘   ⌘   ⌘

Jack Kennedy's meeting with President Eisenhower on December 6, 1960

Image source   http://historyinpieces.com/video/wp-content/blogs.
dir/34/files/2014/07/19601208-Kennedy-and-Eisenhower-57.500.jpg

After President Eisenhower gave his famous speech on the dangers of the military industrial complex, Jack Kennedy had two meetings with President Eisenhower in December 1960 and in January 1961, before Jack became U.S. President in 1961.

During those meetings, President Eisenhower briefed Jack on the dangers posed by the U.S. Military-Industrial complex. Ike also told Jack how he (Eisenhower) had been cut out of the loop for any authority over S-4, Area 51, and other secret military-industrial bases. These bases had been set up to reverse engineer captured alien space crafts as well as alien technology that had been given to the U.S. Military by the aliens – but the President of the United States had NO authority or control over these bases. The discussions lead Jack Kennedy to ask the CIA for full disclosure of all UFO files on November 12, 1963, just 10 days before he was murdered on November 22, 1963.

⌘   ⌘   ⌘

What If?

Conversations with JFK

When you listen to President Eisenhower's famous speech on the dangers of the military-industrial complex, and JFK's "secret societies" speech, you know that both men knew of the threat of

(a) the Military-Industrial complex, and
(b) the Reptilians and the Greys posed to humanity.

Had JFK not been killed, Jack related to me the following events that would have been averted or prevented. As well, he discloses certain projects benefitting humanity that would have been implemented.

1. The United States would have never gone to full scale war with Vietnam, and 42,000 American men and women, and hundreds of thousands of Vietnamese would have never been killed. Ho Chi Minh (the leader of North Vietnam) actually first sought American help in his war of independence from the French, because he truly believed that the U.S. was a great democracy that stood for truth and justice for all. Unfortunately President Truman turned Ho Chi Min down, so he went to the Soviet Union and asked Stalin for help. As a result, North Vietnam became a communist state. Jack would have pulled out all troops by 1966 – he had already issued an order to withdraw troops just before he was murdered in 1963.

2. The moneys that were spent on the Vietnam war would have gone into education and cleaning up the environment, creating a beautiful, peaceful planet.

3. At the time Jack Kennedy was murdered by the CIA, the Mafia, and the private banks of the Federal Reserve, he had sent a French journalist to negotiate with Fidel Castro about normalizing relations between the two countries. By 1966, there would have been peaceful relationships between the U.S. and Cuba. [1]

4. When JFK was murdered on November 22, 1963, his Vice President (Lyndon Baines Johnson) was under investigation for criminal activities (including a possible murder) in Texas. He would have been forced out of office by January 1, 1964. JFK would have found a different Vice President to replace Johnson. He would have easily gone onto a second term as President from 1964 to 1968. Johnson would have

---

[1]   "Kennedy's Last Act: Reaching Out to Cuba – November 20, 1963" at: https://nsarchive.wordpress.com/2013/11/20/kennedys-last-act-reaching-out-to-cuba/

likely ended up in Federal Prison for the rest of his life.[2]

5. By 1966, JFK would have eliminated the Federal Reserve — the U.S. would once again print it's own currency through the United States Treasury, as it did for over 100 years before 1913. The national debt would have been dramatically reduced. The U.S. would be a far more economically and spiritually enlightened country than it is today. [3]

6.   JFK would have purged the CIA of all Nazi influence, especially George Bush Sr. and Allen Dulles.

7. Jack Kennedy ordered the disclosure of all UFO files on November 12, 1963, just 10 days before he was assassinated. With the disclosure of the UFO files from the CIA, JKF would have made it publicly known of the secret deals with the negative Reptilians and Greys extraterrestrials. JFK would have asked the Pleiadies, Valliant Thor, and the Galactic Alliance for spiritual and technological assistance in transforming our planet into a truly beautiful, and harmonious place.

8. By 1966, the cold war with the Soviet Union would have ended. Both countries (with the help of the Pleiadians, Valliant Thor, and the Galactic Alliance) would have entered into a new period of genuine cooperation. The United States would have established diplomatic relations with the People's Republic of China by 1968 – four years before Nixon's effort in 1972.

9. The benevolent Extraterrestrials would have taught us how to provide free energy to all humanity; the use of petroleum as a fuel source would have totally ended by 1970. The planet would be much cleaner, with fewer pollution problems as clean non-polluting energy would have been used. The

---

[2]   Barr McClellan, *Blood, Money, & Power: How LBJ Killed JFK* (2011).
[3]   James L. Paris and Robert G. Yetman Jr., *JFK Assassination: Executive Order 11110 - Did The Fed Kill JFK?* (2015)

Valdez and the Gulf Oil spills would have never happened!

10.   There would have been no Gulf Wars in the 1990s, no war in Iraq with all those people senselessly killed in the 2000s, no war in Syria in the 2010s, no 9/11 in 2001, no wars in Bosnia in the 1990s, no problems with the oil pipeline at Standing Rock in North Dakota, and no world conflicts.

11.   Nuclear power would have been completely outlawed by 1970.   There would have been no Three Mile Island, Chernobyl or Fukushima disasters.   Millions of people would   not   have   died   of   cancer   and   birth   defects.

12.   George Bush Senior would have been arrested and prosecuted for his many crimes against humanity by 1972. He would have spent most of his final years in Federal prison.

13.   JFK's brother (Robert F. Kennedy) would have been elected President in 1968, and would have served two terms until 1976.   Following in the steps of his brother, he would have also been one of the country's greatest Presidents.   Jack says that Richard Nixon would have never become President. Watergate would have never happened.

14.   According to Jack, "Government today would be much cleaner, honest, and far more transparent, as well as smaller." This is because there would be far fewer laws by now (2017). Without the negative influence of the Reptilians, people would know how to act, without the need for laws and control by the state.   There would still be government but its size would be greatly reduced. It's main purpose would be to initiate and maintain relationships with non-terrestrial races.

15. By today (2017), the Earth would be a member of the Galactic Alliance. We would be exchanging Ambassadors with other ET

civilizations. Also money would no longer be used as a medium of exchange. In addition, as on most advanced human planets, people would now be easily living 200+ years, and most people would be able to communicate telepathically. No one would be able to hide the truth or lie to each other, because people would have the ability to read each other's minds. Language would still be used, but it would be secondary. Education would be free and children would be growing up in a world where there was no conflict, no wars, and only peace and harmony.

16. As with most developed human societies outside Earth, all diseases (including cancer) would have been completely eliminated. Large pharmaceutical companies would have also been completely eliminated, as people would be living long, healthy lives.

17. There would still be a small military industrial complex, but their facilities would only be used to manufacture off planet spacecraft used for peaceful exploration and scientific research. Any defense needs would be provided by membership in the Galactic Alliance.

18. The planet would have ascended into the Fifth Dimension, where people would realize we are all part of the creator, and we are all one.

19. Poverty would have been completely eliminated.

20. Genetically modified food would have never been created. GMO food would not exist today.

21. Gary Sotello (the real name for Barrack Obama) would have never become U.S. President. Jack said Sotello/Obama is a creation of (and controlled by) the CIA, and secret government.

22. The regular killing and cloning of high U.S. Government officials would have never happened. Jack says when he was murdered on November 22, 1963, it was really messy. Jack says

that it's much easier nowadays to simply kill a president and replace him or her with clone, than it is to murder a president in a public, as was done when he was murdered on November 22, 1963. (See also discussion of President Jimmy Carter, below)

For example, Jack said that President Obama was actually murdered in January 2013, just after he was elected to his second term. He was taken to Camp David (where a large cloning facility existed underground until just recently). Obama was then murdered with an injection of a blue fluid filled with poison. When Obama's spirit left his body, the scientists at this underground facility at Camp David extracted his personality. Once extracted, they forced it into another biological clone.

Jack says Obama wanted to do some good things for the United States and the world. However, negative elements within the U.S. Government decided that it would be much easier to simply kill the real Obama, and replace him with a clone. They decided that this would make it much easier to control him. During his second term as President, Obama would often star off into space. Jack said since January 2013, Obama has existed only as a clone. This is why President Obama always talks with a teleprompter; he is very controlled and does not have any free will to say anything on his own.

This cloning technology has been given to some negative elements within the U.S. Government from the Reptilians. The Reptilians pride themselves on being master geneticists, tinkering with life and genetics. Jack says it is very easy for negative elements within the U.S. Government to kill and clone anyone they wish. However, there is good news -- Jack also says that all the cloning facilities at Camp David and other places have been destroyed since last year.

A good psychic can easily tell the difference between a real human and a clone by looking at their auras. A real human has a soul and many different auras and chakras. A real human also exists in the Third Dimension. However, a clone can only exist in the higher levels of the Second Dimension – they do not have chakras. They only have a dull white light at the very top of their head. They are a biological entity, without a real soul.

As another example, Jack said that President Jimmy Carter was also killed and cloned during the week of April 13 to April 21, 1979 when he visited his home in Plains, Georgia. Among several other reasons, negative elements within the U.S. Government decided to kill and clone him after President Carter asked for disclosure of all UFO files from the CIA.

In 1969, President Carter saw a UFO first hand, and reported it in 1973. While he was campaigning in 1976, Carter declared that, if elected, he would "make every piece of information this country has about UFO sightings available to the public and scientists."[4]

So soon after he was elected President, Carter met with George Bush Sr. (the then head of the CIA) for 45 minutes, and asked for UFO disclosure on November 19, 1976. Carter reportedly said, "I want to have the information that we have on UFOs and extraterrestrial intelligence. I want to know about this as President."[5]

Even though Carter had had a 30 year interest in UFOs, after April 1979, he lost all interest. He never again requested UFO disclosure from the CIA after April 1979. Jack says that in every picture of Carter before April 13, 1979, his hair is parted to his left. However, in every picture after April 21, 1979, his hair is parted to the right. Jack says that it is impossible for someone to change the parting of their hair from one side to another in one week – especially when a man has parted his hair on one side for over fifty years.

---

[4]   http://www.timcolemanmedia.com/index.php/articles/ufos/76-presidents-and-ufos
[5]   https://www.democraticunderground.com/discuss/duboard.php?az=view_
all&address=104x1956796

The following pictures illustrate this comment:

https://catalog.archives.gov/id/184311 4/10/79
President Carter's hair is parted to his left (not cloned)

Jimmy Carter entering presidential helicopter,
Hair parted on his left (not cloned)
https://catalog.archives.gov/id/184343
4/13/79

4/21/79 Carter leaving Georgia after visit to this home town of Plains, GA: Hair parted on his right (cloned)
https://catalog.archives.gov/id/184515

5/3/79 Jimmy Carter – Alaska Briefing. Hair clearly parted to his right (cloned): https://catalog.archives.gov/id/184692

22.   There would be complete UFO disclosure, and we would be now exchanging Ambassadors with other advanced civilizations beyond this planet.   The secrecy around Extraterrestrial Life beyond this planet would have ended. The Reptilians and their negative allies would no longer be able to control our governments and corporations.

As an example, in 2015, President Obama was interviewed by comedian Jerry Kimmel on the NBC TV network. During that interview, Mr. Kimmel told President Obama that the first thing he would have done if he had become President was to find out if UFOs are real. President Obama's response was very interesting. Kimmel wanted to know whether Obama had tried to get to the bottom of the "UFO files" about the mysterious desert region known as Area 51. According to the LA Times and Mr. Michael Salla, Obama joked, "the aliens won't let it happen," Obama joked.

"You'd reveal all their secrets. They exercise strict control over us."

"But President Clinton once said he'd checked on the matter and found nothing," Kimmel protested. "That's what we're instructed to say," Obama responded.

Obama's comments come only one month after Podesta claimed his biggest failure for 2014 was: "Once again not securing the disclosure of the UFO files." Normally, President Obama blinks a lot when he talks (which is indicative of lying), but this time, he looked straight at Mr. Kimmel and (without blinking), and said "they keep a tight rein on us; they tell us to tell the public that there is nothing at Area 51, and that they control the world." Although Mr. Kimmel took his comments as a joke, Dr. Michael Salla had the video of President Obama's interview analyzed by some police detectives. They found that he was actually telling the truth and was very serious – see: "Obama admits space aliens control USA: Was he joking?"[1]

[1]   http://exopolitics.org/obama-admits-space-aliens-control-usa-was-he-joking/

However, the controls exercised by the Reptilians and negative elements within the U.S. Government are slowly being taken away, so we can have our free will back. Because the true nature of humanity is to be kind, benevolent, and loving, Jack Kennedy says that it is the destiny of planet Earth to become a peaceful, loving, and benevolent place. He also says that this planet is slated for ascension into the higher dimensions, where we will all create a true paradise!

We on this Earth had a chance to make this wonderful transformation into the higher dimensions when Jack was President in the early 1960s. Jack tried to abolish the Federal Reserve, rein in the Central Intelligence Agency, and tried to approach the Soviet Union to establish a joint space program and true collaboration (instead of conflict and competition).

He says that history moves in cycles. The same cycles which were present in the 1950s and early 1960s for a much better and happier planet have come back again some 60 years later. Jack says that it is our destiny to live in true peace and harmony, and now, the entire planet is shifting rapidly into the higher dimensions.

⌘   ⌘   ⌘

If JFK was the President Now

If he were the President now, Jack Kennedy told me he would do the following:

1.   Have the U.S. Treasury immediately start issuing what he would call "United States Notes"; he would abolish the Federal Reserve by the end of 2017.

2.   Abolish the "common core" educational system that was instituted by President Obama in 45 states; In his own words, Jack calls the system a "stupid idea," designed to dumb down American kids, bringing educational levels down to the Third World throughout the United States. Jack says we can do much better than that. When he was President, the educational system in the United States was one of the best. However with this common core system, the U.S. educational system is now one of the world's worst. This is because many math, science, English literature, and art classes (which encourage intuition and creative thinking) have been eliminated.

3.   Pull all troops out of Afghanistan, which he calls another "Vietnam in the Middle East." The only reason we are in Afghanistan is because the CIA makes money off the drug trade, bringing in heroin from Afghanistan directly into Mexico, and then smuggling it across the Mexican border into the United States. Jack says that this is the REAL reason why the Mexican border does not have better security. He says if they did close off the border, the CIA would no-longer be able to transport their drugs into the United States. The CIA started its drug operations during the Vietnam War, by bringing in heroin from the so called "Golden Triangle" in South East Asia. Jack refers to the as CIA a "lawless agency" that he would (in his words) "completely dismantle" if he were President now.

4. Cut off all funding for ISIS in the Middle East. He says that both Obama and Senator McCain funded and started ISIS in 2013 as a way to destabilize Syria. If US funding were cut off from ISIS, they could be stopped tomorrow.

5. Immediately put a moratorium to all new nuclear power plant construction in the US. He would order a halt to any current construction of the new nuclear power plants like the ones Obama ordered in 2013 in Georgia. He said this construction is a tremendous waste of money! He would also order the immediate testing of air and water off the U.S. West Coast for radiation. Obama's decision to stop radiation at all federal testing facilities on the U.S. West Coast in 2013 was (in Jack's words) "dead wrong". Obama's executive order to increase the amount of so called "allowable radiation" from nuclear power plants to 10,000 rads per year was also "dead wrong."[1]

Jack would immediately rescind Obama's order — he would reduce the amount of so called acceptable radiation exposure to 100 rads per year, in line with Switzerland's radiation protocols.

6. Immediately put the United States on a path to clean energy sources, and mandate the energy efficiency of new cars produced in the United States to 50 mpg by next year.

7. Immediately order the disclosure of all UFO files in the hands of the CIA, especially all files and information related to the Secret Space Program. Jack would also order disclosure of all the secret human slave labor camps run by Boeing and other companies in the Corporate Global Conglomerate based on Mars.

8. Immediately rescind the presidential order by President Bill Clinton in 1996 — this allowed Monsanto the right to use Genetically Modified Corn and other GMO foods.

1   http://www.activistpost.com/2013/04/obama-approves-epas-higher-radiation.html

According to Jack, these foods are "dangerous" and "unhealthy."

9.   Immediately contact the Pleiadians and the Galactic Alliance, and ask them for their help in transforming the United States and the planet into a far better and happier place, with the elimination of disease and poverty.

Jack commented he can speak the truth from the other side. "What are they going to do to me now? Kill me? Ha, ha, ha!"

⌘   ⌘   ⌘

⌘   ⌘   ⌘

Dr. Masaru Emoto

Contact with the Great Spirits

After speaking to Jack Kennedy, I was very fortunate to come to in contact with Dr. Masaru Emoto.

Before he passed away on October 17, 2014, Dr. Emoto was one of the world's great spiritual people. He proved our thoughts influence and create our physical reality. Dr. Emoto found positive thoughts can create beautiful water crystals, while negative thoughts can create ugly and disorderly crystals. These pictures from his beautiful book, Messages from Water show how our positive words such "love and gratitude" form coherent crystalline structures, where negative words such as "hate and fear" form incoherent structures.

The crystal below is formed when the word, "you fool," is written on a glass of water:

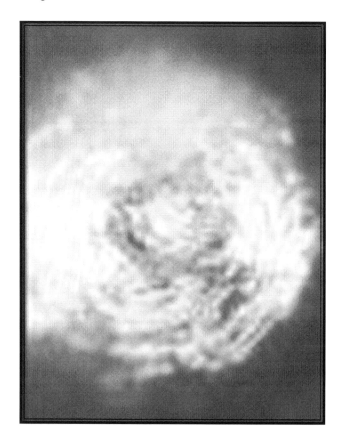

In addition, this water crystal below is formed when the word "evil" is written on a glass of water:

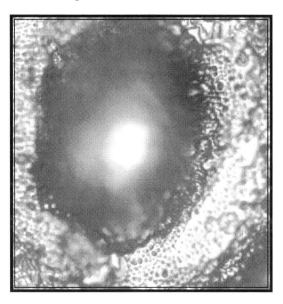

By comparison, this beautiful crystal is formed by the words of "Love and Gratitude." Of all the water crystals, the ones produced by the words "Love and Gratitude" are the most beautiful.

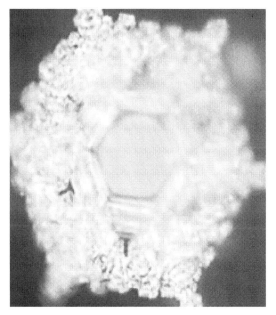

Dr. Emoto founded the "Emoto Peace Project" in 2005, with his famous speech at the United Nations, where he proposed teaching the children of the world the valuable lessons of love and gratitude. Once children learned, he proposed they would want to create a planet based on harmonious relationships, cooperation, love and gratitude later in life when they grew up to be adults.

See: www.emotopeaceproject.me and www.emotopeaceproject.net

Since our bodies are 70 percent water, and the planet is also 70 percent water, he believed we are just like our beautiful planet. Water is the life blood of planet Earth. Dr. Emoto also found that water has memory. Just the simple act of writing the words "love and gratitude" on a bottle of radioactive water caused all traces of radiation to disappear within 48 hours! This occurs because water has memory and radiation cannot exist in water with "love and gratitude."

Dr. Emoto stated we are powerful sovereign spiritual beings and we can create the kind of world we want! Teaching children these lessons is the best way to make this world a better place.

Today his work, the Emoto Peace Project, is carried on by Michiko Hayashi, who was Dr. Emoto's assistant for 10 years, before he passed away in 2014. Fluent in English, Japanese, Spanish, and other languages, Michiko spreads the positive messages of love and gratitude in a wonderful children's book called The Messages from Water. The book is distributed for free to children around the world by her and her office in Tokyo.

According to Dr. Emoto, to change the world into a more positive and loving place now, we only needed to change one percent. Most people of Earth (80 percent) are neutral regarding the future, with an additional 10 percent positive, and the other 10 percent negative. If we can change only one percent and combine it with the other 10 percent positive, we will tip the balance of humanity on this planet and create a more positive and brighter future.

The great news is this one percent did in fact change into the positive in September 2016, when powerful energy waves hit the Earth from September 5 to 15, and then again on September 22 and 23, 2016. This is what these powerful energy waves looked like when they hit the planet:[1]

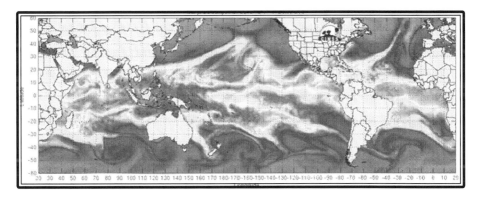

The months of October and November, 2016 were quiet months, followed by another energy wave from December 21, 2016 to January 7, 2017. During Easter week, starting on April 11, 2017, there were another series of positive energy waves hitting planet Earth lasting several weeks, raising the Schumann Resonance Frequency of the planet to over 36![2]

During May 2017, the Schumann Resonance Frequency has now gone up to 120 Hertz! By the time this book is published, I am sure that the frequency of the planet will be even higher.

These are the first of many positive energy waves which are raising the vibratory levels of the planet, helping to transform the Earth into a 5th dimensional world! According to Nostradamus, this process

[1]   http://www.ascensionwithearth.com/2016/12/large-wave-of-energy-from-unknown.html
[2]   http://prepareforchange.net/2017/02/02/humans-are-waking-up-for-first-time-in-recorded-history-schumann-resonance-jumping-to-36/

will continue until the year 2038, when the process will be complete.

Before Dr. Emoto passed away on October 17, 2014, I interviewed him on my radio show on July 25, 2014 from 3 pm to 4 pm (Pacific Standard Time). At 3:30 pm, during that interview, I thanked Dr. Emoto for his wonderful research — I then asked him if positive thoughts could help bring about world peace. He said positive thoughts should have the same effect, as on the water crystals.

So during my radio show, we did an intention experiment where we sent love and light to the Palestinians and the Israelis. During that interview, we also asked for the Palestinians and the Israelis to have a 12 hour cease fire so that they could provide food and medical care to the wounded. After the show, I went to where I was staying and just as I turned on CNN on the TV at 8:30 pm that evening, the Palestinian and Israeli government had spontaneously agreed to have a 12 hour cease fire to provide food and medical supplies to the wounded. Our intention experiment worked! And the wonderful lesson that I learned from Dr. Emoto that day was we are all powerful spiritual beings meant to create a much better and happier planet!

There was another lesson from that experience as well. When I reviewed the audio from the program, all of the show was there on the recording, except for the part at 3:30 pm where Dr. Emoto and I had sent love and light to the Palestinians. Something had replaced the recording where we had done our intention experiment with the sound of papers being shuffled! It's strange to have the shuffling of papers, in the middle of my radio show without anything else for about 4 or 5 minutes.

When I asked my benevolent friends off planet what had happened, I was told the Reptilians are technologically advanced and had altered the recording of the show, so the recording would be just the shuffling of papers, and no mention of our intention experiment. They do not want humanity to know that we are powerful spiritual beings capable of creating our own reality and bringing peace and harmony to this world! (See July 25, 2014 interview with Dr. Emoto at: http://outofthisworld1150.com/guests/emoto-peace-project/.)

Of course, a lot has changed since Dr. Emoto passed away on October 17th of 2014. Since 2014, the Galactic Alliance has stepped in and provided a lot of protection for many light workers around the world. Also, I am told that many negative entities have been driven off the planet — our future is very bright! The Reptilians, their friends and negative allies do not want people to realize that we are slated for ascension into the higher dimensions. The message I received over and over again is that our future is very bright. However, we have to work with the Supreme Being or the Prime Creator to create a bright, beautiful, and loving planet.

One of the other fascinating things that Dr. Emoto noted was we human are 70 percent water, just as the Earth is 70 percent water. He referred to water as "God" — the life blood of our planet. This is a very important and profound statement.

⌘   ⌘   ⌘

Fracking

Fracking is a procedure for underground petroleum exploration and extraction which ruins and pollutes the water used in the process. The more we allow fracking to continue, the more damage we do to our beautiful planet. I am told by my friends off planet the Reptilians running the U.S. Government want to destroy the water on this planet in this way. This is also why the U.S. and other governments have done NOTHING about Fukushima and the radiation there. The only work that has been done to help the people and children of Fukushima has been largely done by the Emoto Peace Project, and a few private nonprofit organizations — see: www.emotopeaceproject.net and www.emotopeaceproject.me

Because water has memory, in the future, we will be able to make organic computers which will have water memory storage. According to Professor Albert Einstein, these computers will be partially organic, with memory based on EZ water which will have an extra oxygen molecule, H_3O_2.

The additional oxygen molecule will enable the water to store much more information in a far more compact form than our present computers.

According to Matias de Stefano, water was used to store information during Atlantian times. In interviews on both my radio and television shows, Matias said that the information from Atlantis is actually stored in the water of the world's oceans. He also said that one day, we will be access that information. Matias is a young man who has detailed, specific memories of his life in Atlantis 12,500 years ago — see his interview at: http://outofthisworld1150.com/guests/matias-de-stefano/

⌘ ⌘ ⌘

Everything is "Hado" or Vibration

During this ascension process, it is very important to realize that this planet and many people on it are headed to the 5th Dimension, and beyond. In the 5th Dimension, Dr. Emoto tells me that "thoughts are things." As part of this ascension process, Dr. Emoto emphasizes everything in this Third Dimension has "hado" or vibration. As the Earth ascends into the 5th Dimension, our thoughts will become more critical. Thoughts are things in the 5th Dimension – and we have to be very careful that we think only positive thoughts. This is because our thoughts in the 5th Dimension will materialize faster and faster into the 3rd Dimension. Dr. Emoto says by raising your vibration you can change the world! As he discovered in the late 1990s, when you can raise a person's vibration, you can also activate a self-healing process.

To help heal people, Dr. Emoto devised a special Hado vibration machine to determine the correct vibration (or hado) for a person to help cure and heal almost any spiritual or physical condition. During his lifetime, he was able to successfully treat over 10,000 people using his Hado vibration machines from the 1990s to when he passed away in 2014. Often, he found that many illnesses and spiritual problems came not only from this life, but from the lives of a person's ancestors (previous lives) going back up to seven generations. In effect, the person was paying in this life for the past karmic debt of their ancestors.

Both Corey Goode and Randy Cramer of the Secret Space Program told me on the air during my Out of this World Radio shows in 2015 and 2016 that the American Secret Space Program uses vibration treat illness. They have medical clinics on the dark side of the moon which can heal any physical disease, including cancer. If a person had cancer, they would just have that person lie on a table and a computer would program the correct vibration for that person to get rid of their cancer. Both Cory Goode and Randy

Cramer said that the machines were 100 percent effective. See the interview: http://outofthisworld1150.com/guests/randy-kramer/ and also: http://outofthisworld1150.com/guests/corey-goode/

Thus, Corey Goode, Randy Cramer, and Dr. Emoto are all saying the same thing — i.e., that vibration is the key. With higher vibration, you can heal the sick, clean up pollution and make this world a happier and more beautiful place!

As an example, one of the amazing experiments that Dr. Emoto did in 1999 was to take a bottle of radioactive water and to place a beautiful "Love and Gratitude" crystal on the bottle, with the words "Love and Gratitude" written on the bottle. He found that within 48 hours, ALL of the radiation in the water had completely disappeared! The water had resonated with the words love and gratitude on the bottle. See: http://emotopeaceproject.blogspot. jp/2012/10/please-help-children-of-fukushima_22.html

Dr. Emoto wrote, "I have been studying about water and Hado for the past 25 years. In October 1999 when the Tokaimura radiation leak accident happened, I took a crystal photograph of the water from a well located only 400 meters away from the scene of the accident."

The crystal pictured below represents a water sample affected by the radioactive material:

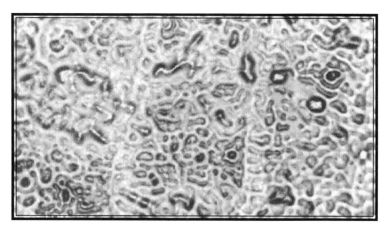

Dr. Emoto was "not surprised to see that the damaged crystal image from the radiation contaminated water changed to a beautiful crystal image, when I imprinted the Hado of "Love and Gratitude" into the water that was previously contaminated

with radiation. The fact that this beautiful diamond shaped water crystal formed from the same irradiated water after the Hado of love & gratitude was imprinted means the Law of Nature settled into the water, that is, the influence of a radioactive material has been successfully removed." By "Law of Nature," I think Dr. Emoto meant a natural law of the universe.[1]

In another experiment, with the help of Buddhist Priests, Dr. Emoto said prayers at the Fujiwara Dam outside Tokyo. These pictures show the water before (left) and after (right) prayers at the Dam:

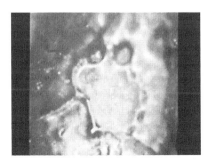 

---

[1]   http://emotopeaceproject.blogspot.jp/2012/10/please-help-children-of-fukushima_22.html

Dr. Emoto also experimented with a group of 500 people to send positive thoughts and prayers to the water sitting on the desk of a colleague in Los Angeles, over 5000 miles away. The result of these prayers was to transfer the water into these beautiful water crystals![2]   (see picture below)

Projecting thoughts of 'Love and Gratitude" would be a very simple, yet effective solution to the radiation leaking into the Pacific Ocean from Fukushima, as well as the radioactive water leaking into the Columbia River in Washington State from the Hanford Nuclear Waste Dump site. Dr. Emoto felt the only barrier to implementing such a novel solution would be the scientists and government administrators — because they would probably not believe that such a solution would work! (see: Out of this World Radio interview on June 3, 2016 for Professor Gerald Pollack at: http://outofthisworld1150.com/guests/gerald-pollack/) In other words, their belief system would be the only barrier to cleaning up Fukushima and Hanford.

Dr. Emoto said he came from the Pleadians to this planet approximately 52,000 years, or 720 life-times ago to raise

[2]   http://www.masaru-emoto.net/english/water-crystal.html

consciousness and make this world a better place.   He is now in the 5th Dimension, and is working with scientists from the Pleadians in the 5th and 6th Dimensions to clean up the water of the Earth.   He says that we are getting help from the Pleadians, the Hollow Earth, and other members of the Galactic Alliance to clean up the water of this beautiful planet.

⌘   ⌘   ⌘

⌘   ⌘   ⌘

The Galactic Alliance

Contact with the Great Spirits

Through my friendship with Scott Lemriel, author of the Seres Agenda, I was put into contact with Ambassador Torwellian of the Galactic Alliance about three years ago. The Galactic Alliance is a benevolent alliance of 435 million planets, in this one third of the Milky Way Galaxy. The Alliance numbers approximately 7 trillion entities; they are mostly (but not all) human. We are seeded from them, and look like them, because the human species is extremely old.

The Galactic Alliance is between 50,000 and 100,000 years ahead of us technologically. There are also between 30,000 and 50,000 years ahead of us spiritually. The Pleadians and the people of the Hollow Earth are all members of the Galactic Alliance. Their formal name is the "Galactic Alliance of Interdimensional Free Worlds."

The good news for humanity is that we are now getting real help from the benevolent Galactic Alliance and the Hollow Earth. As one of many examples, during the spring of 2014, a huge radioactive plume of water was headed from Fukushima across the Pacific directly for Seattle on the U.S. West Coast. The plume contained 10 times more radiation than all the atomic bombs dropped since Hiroshima and Nagasaki.

I became concerned at these reports, and so I had the water off Seattle and the Washington Coast tested for radiation in April and May 2014. In 2013, President Obama (under control by the Reptilians and other negative entities) had shut down all eight Federal radiation monitoring stations. Washington Governor Inslee had done the same thing, so no radiation testing was being done by any state or federal agency in Washington State.

During this time, President Obama also raised the so called "acceptable" radiation exposure from nuclear accidents by an incredible 10 times, to 10,000 rads, guaranteeing that no one who was exposed to radiation would have any legal redress in the U.S. Court system. (Extensive documentation on this is found at: http://www.agreenroadjournal.com/2014/01/epa-covered-up-and-hid-fukushima.html)

Because no testing was being done either by the federal or state government in Washington State, I had to have the testing done privately. I also asked California Governor Brown's office in Sacramento for help. In 2014, his office agreed to do all the radiation testing I wanted for free, since neither Obama nor Inslee (who campaigned for office claiming that he was an "environmentalist") would do any testing. I want to thank Governor Brown so much for doing these radiation tests.

When the test results came back, it showed that ALL of the radiation from Fukushima had completely disappeared!

(See test results attached in Appendix B.) When California Governor Brown found out the same thing after he tested the waters off the California coast May 2016, on June 1st, 2014, he issued a press release celebrating the fact that the radiation from Fukushima had completely disappeared! However, this news was only broadcast on television, radio, and newspapers within the State of California. No mention of this wonderful news was ever broadcast or printed anywhere outside of California. See copies of test results in Appendix B.

Since then, I have received messages from the Galactic Alliance that we on are co-creators with the Supreme Being (or God) in creating a beautiful, bright, and happy planet! They (and the advanced civilizations in the Hollow Earth) are the ones who have been cleaning up Fukushima and the Pacific Ocean. To the Galactic Alliance, cleaning up radiation is a very old technological process, which was used most recently 52,000 years ago by the Pleadians, after a civil war where millions died as a result of nuclear weapons. This is why the use of nuclear technology is absolutely illegal outside of this planet today on other advanced human civilizations throughout the Galaxy.

⌘   ⌘   ⌘

Ho'oponopono Water Prayer for Fukushima

When I visited James Guilland's ranch at Mt. Adams WA in July 2015, I was given the message that we are all very powerful spiritual beings. Our friends in the Galactic Alliance told me they want us to work with them and the Supreme Being in cleaning up Fukushima.

The radiation from Fukushima has not been completely cleaned up by the Galactics and the people of the Hollow Earth; they want us to do our part in the cleanup. "We will never learn from our mistakes, unless we play a role in correcting them." They need our positive energy and prayers to help clean up Fukushima.

In 2015 when I was given this message by Dr. Emoto and the Galactic Alliance to send prayers, I was also given the message to send healing love and light to the people and especially the children of Fukushima. Dr. Emoto wants everyone reading this book to say this prayer three times every day:

"Water we are sorry,
Water please forgive us,
Water we thank you, and
Water we love you."

Dr. Emoto requests that as you say the prayer, please send golden light and love to the children and people of Fukushima.

This is one of the many ways each of us can clean up Fukushima. As Jack Kennedy has said, we are very powerful spiritual beings; we are here to help create a beautiful, harmonious and loving Earth.

This prayer was Dr. Emoto's favorite healing prayer which was based on Ho'oponopono, a powerful ancient Hawaiian prayer that was used for healing. The literal translation of Ho'oponopono is "to make (ho'o) right (pono) right (pono)" — the prayer is used to correct relationship problems.

In the past, a kahuna or Hawaiian doctor would be called into a family situation to uncover problems, practice forgiveness and release each other from recriminations, grudges and guilt. "They knew that conflicts and grudges eventually cause disease" according to Dr. Betty W. Phillips.[1]

⌘   ⌘   ⌘

[1]   www.bettyphillipspsychology.com/id169.html

⌘   ⌘   ⌘

We Are All Powerful
Spiritual Beings

Messages from the Galaxy

Our Home - The Milky Way Galaxy

We are all powerful spiritual beings. In fact, other extraterrestrial groups outside of this planet call us "genetic royalty." We have the strands of 22 different ET races within us, even though we are human. Our DNA has been tinkered with for many thousands of years. Jack Kennedy says that if he had lived, we would be exchanging Ambassadors with other benevolent ET races by now. This would give us the opportunity to meet some of our progenitors. We as humans would have a life span of several hundred years instead of the current world average of 67.2 years.

There are two main Extraterrestrial groups where Earth is located in this part of the Milky Way Galaxy. One is positive and feeds off of love and service to others (which is the Galactic Alliance). The other is negative and feeds off of war and hate, and is service to self (which is called the Reptilians).

There is a lot to tell about the history of these two groups, but the short version is that there was a war between the two groups about 500,000 years ago. This was when the planet Maldek was destroyed, and Mars lost much of its atmosphere. The asteroid belt just beyond Mars is the remnants of the planet Maldek.

During this war a half a million years ago, the Galactic Alliance won the war. The two sides then signed a treaty in which they essentially agreed on noninterference with the people of Earth, in exchange for each side being allowed to have bases here on the planet for scientific research. The Reptilians established bases in the Congo in Africa and in Brazil in the Amazon. The Galactic Alliance established bases in Norway, and in Mt. Shasta in California, among other places. However, since the treaty was signed, there has been an active cold war going on between the two groups and still goes on, even today. The treaty has been broken many, many times by the Reptilians.

The Earth is located on the outskirts of one of the arms of

the Milky Way Galaxy and right on the path of many trading routes. The transformation happening now on our planet is being watched by the entire universe. The Galactic Alliance is looking forward to the time when Earth is welcomed as a full member. According to Nostradamus, this transformation will be complete by 2038 A.D. When complete, Earth will become a more beautiful planet. We will also be living in peace and harmony with all of humanity and with other races as well.

The Earth is located at an arm on the far left side of the Milky Way Galaxy.. Our planet has been in relative isolation for the past 500,000 years. However, this is ending now. Very soon, we will become members of the Galactic Alliance.

One of the primary ET representatives I have been in contact with is Ambassador Torwellian of the Galactic Alliance. Ambassador Torwellian is a wonderful person, who looks like he is in his early 30s in Earth years. In actual fact he is about 10,000 years old .[1]

---

[1]   Vesna Perkorva (from Croatia) – Ambassador Torwellian from April 1st, 2017 email

I have been very fortunate in that the Galactics have been providing several spacecraft as protection for me whenever I go anywhere. Here is a photo of a spacecraft that appeared over my Galactic Wisdom Conference in Olympia, Washington in June 2016:

At night, they usually appear in the same five light point formation, with a larger point of the light in the middle. During the day, their craft often appears with a blue tint, as in the picture above.

Ambassador Torwellian is from the Seres, a very ancient race that has been around for billions of years. He himself is 10,000 years old, and if he so chooses, can live up to 25,000 years. According to Ambassador Torwellian, on most advanced human planets outside Earth, people live an average of 1000 years. They remember all of their past lives, why they were born, and what lessons they should learn. On most human planets, they communicate telepathically. Money is not used as a medium of exchange. Ambassador Torwellian says that money is a Reptilian concept. Included in the Galactic Alliance are the

Pleadians, the Arcturians, the Andromedans, the benevolent civilizations of the Inner Earth, and many other groups.

The Reptilians (and their controlled robotic slave species, the Greys and the Tall Whites) look at humans like cattle or chickens. They are a resource driven species; they view the Earth and its inhabitants as "resources" to be exploited and used. The Reptilians also consider themselves the top of the evolutionary chain, and are highly technological.   They look down upon humans, who they consider "inferior" because we are an evolving species. In their view, we have not reached the "pinnacle" of our evolution. The Reptilians arrogantly consider themselves to be "perfect."

According to my Galactic friends, about 15,000 years ago, the Reptilians interfered with our human evolution on Earth by interbreeding.   They created hybrid Reptilian/human "royal families" or "royalty." Princess Diana referred to the British Royal Family as "the lizard people." The so called "royal families" on Earth are Reptilian in nature; "royalty" and hierarchal societies do not exist in other advanced human planets outside of Earth. "Royalty" only exists in Reptilian society where there is a clear hierarchy. There is no such thing as "free will" in Reptilian society, because everything is controlled. Among the Reptilians, there is only "duty" and "honor" among their Reptilian "royal families."

In Star Trek, there was the policy of noninterference – that policy is generally true here on planet Earth, with several important exceptions. The Earth is itself is on a trade route between other star systems in the Milky Way Galaxy. This planet has many time and dimensional portals. In addition to having tremendous resources, the planet itself is very valuable to the Reptilians and their allies.

Because the Reptilians are a resource driven species, they seek to conquer other worlds and other planets through trade and persuasion. They consider themselves the smartest and most cunning species in the universe. Their nervous system operates three times faster than our own. They are very psychic. They can read your mind before you even act. They are a formidable adversary. However, they are cut off from the Prime Creator — they must conquer other worlds in order to survive.

The Reptilians and their allies (the Greys and the Tall Whites) are doing to Earth now what they have done in 22 other star systems. In these other star systems, they first contact the elites of a planet and offer them special benefits, in exchange for reducing the planet's population. After they have reduced a planet's population by 90 or 95 percent, they have what they consider a "manageable slave population" to extract resources. After taking out all the resources, they then destroy the entire planet with an anti-matter bomb.

The Reptilians installed a "doomsday bomb" the size of half of a railroad box car during the 1950s after they successfully negotiated an illegal agreement with U.S. President Dwight D. Eisenhower. The agreement allowed them to "abduct" and "study" humans. In exchange, they gave the U.S. some of their technology to fight the Soviets during the cold war.

Because of this bomb, the Galactic Alliance has to go slow in transforming the planet, or else the Reptilians could try and detonate this bomb to destroy the Earth. But the Galactics are working hard behind the scenes to help us as much as possible in every way they can. I know with their help, we will be able turn this planet around.

When U.S. President Eisenhower was negotiating with the Reptilians, the Reptilians were also negotiating with the Soviets. The Reptilians offered the Soviets the same deal, where Reptilian technology would be shared with the Soviet military. In exchange, the Reptilians would be allowed to abduct and "study" humans. Unfortunately, both the Soviets and the Americans agreed to let the Reptilians and the Greys abduct humans, in exchange for their technology. As a result of that illegal agreement with the Americans, 6 million people from the United States since the 1950s have been abducted by the Greys and the Reptilians. Only one and a half million people have been returned — the rest have either been eaten by the Reptilians (human flesh is considered a great delicacy), or sold into slavery. Fortunately, the abductions have been stopped recently by the Galactic Alliance.

The Greys (which are a slave species of the Reptilians) have come to this planet in particular to "harvest" our human DNA in an effort to save their own species from extinction. As Ambassador Torwellian has explained, the Greys suffer from what is called "progenesis", which is a gradual deterioration of their DNA.

They do not reproduce like we humans do; instead, they clone themselves. The problem with repeated cloning is that their DNA has broken down. It's like a picture in which you make a copy from a copy over and over again – eventually, the image of the picture is not recognizable. According to my Galactic friends, the Greys themselves were captured many thousands of years ago by the Reptilians. Once captured, they were genetically altered to become a slave/servant race to the Reptilians.

There is no free will among the Reptilians and the Greys. The whole concept of "free will" is completely foreign to them, because in their culture, they have to control everything, and everything is controlled.

Ambassador Torwellian believes this is why many negative elements within the American Government want to "control" and "monitor" everything, because much of the U.S. Government is in turn controlled by the Reptilians and the Greys. According to Alex Collier (an Andromedan Galaxy contactee), the Reptilians can time travel. According to Alex, they have learned that under one time line, we humans on Earth kick out the

Reptilians from this part of the universe 300 years from now. Alex says they have come from the future to change history.[1]

In addition to adding genetic vitality to their species, the Greys have embarked upon a hybridization program where they have tried to create hybrid human/grey aliens. There are several reasons for this hybridization program, including the fact that the Earth's atmosphere is too rich in oxygen for Greys. However, the Grey/Human hybrids can survive and prosper in our atmosphere. As Professor David Jacobs of Temple University has noted, they are now releasing these hybrid Grey/Human aliens into the general population of the United States and other countries.[2]

These hybrids may "look" human, but they are actually part Grey/human hybrids, controlled by the Greys and the Reptilians. The Greys are doing the same thing that was done to them many thousands of years ago by the Reptilians – they are creating a controllable species. However, because their species is genetically dying, this attempt will ultimately fail.

One negative outgrowth of the Reptilians and the Greys has been the secret chem trail spraying program. The secret chemtrail program is being done by the Reptilian controlled U.S. Government, as well as by the Reptilians themselves in the Earth's atmosphere. The program is generally not reported in the U.S. Mass Media, since 90 percent of the mass media in the United States is controlled by only about six companies, nearly all of which have direct ties to the U.S. military industrial complex – the same complex that President Eisenhower gravely warned all of us about in 1959.[3]

The planes generally spray aluminum, barium, strontium, and sulphur, in addition to numerous biological agents which many

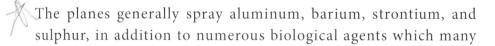

[1] Alex Collier, *Standing Ground*, published in 1996 – available at: http://www.alexcollier.org/alex-collier-defending-sacred-ground-1996/.
[2]   http://outofthisworld1150.wixsite.com/outofthisworld/david-jacobs
[3]   http://www.eisenhower.archives.gov/research/online_documents/farewell_address.html

think cause Morgellon's disease and other health problems. As one example, in one rural area of Eastern Washington in Moses Lake (where I lived until October 2014), the U.S. Navy was spraying large amounts of these chemicals every other day, sometimes within about 40 or 50 yards of the ground in Orion P-130 aircraft. The planes flew so close to the ground that you could easily see the pilots of these craft (see pictures below):

Photograph of chem trails being sprayed by a U.S. Navy plane.

Chem Trails

While living in Moses Lake, Washington, I had the local lake water, air, and fish tested for heavy metals, and what I found was very alarming! (See Appendix C: Chem Trail Tests in Moses Lake WA.) In the tests that I had run, the aluminum content of the air was up to 10,000 times of what it should be, with other rates for barium and strontium up to 6000 and 8000 times of what their rates should have been, as well as high rates for Sulphur.

In the fish from Moses Lake itself, the rates were also extremely high, making the fish unsuitable and dangerous to eat. The U.S. Navy was dumping literally tons of Sulphur into the atmosphere during the summer of 2014 at the same time that local temperatures soared to 110 and 115 degrees F., and beyond. This was an apparent attempt to make outside air temperatures even hotter. The Sulphur undoubtedly raised air temperatures while many forest fires were burning. Many houses were lost during these fires. I think the Navy and the U.S. Government (and the Reptilians) are partially responsible for this destruction. Bill Gates actually paid hundreds of millions of dollars for the Sulphur to be aerially sprayed at the same time that temperatures in Eastern Washington were very, very hot.[1]

Why would the U.S. Navy and Bill Gates spray these chemicals in Eastern Washington in general and in Moses Lake in particular?

My Galactic friends suggest that the Reptilian controlled U.S. Navy is spraying these chemicals to terra form the planet. They want to make it more friendly to the Reptilians and less friendly to humans, all the while decreasing the human population through disease and cancer. I am told that it is no accident that Draco, the home planet of the Reptilians, has a temperature of

---

[1]   http://www.geoengineeringwatch.org/bill-gates-funds-scheme-to-spray-artificial-planet-cooling-sulfur-particles-into-atmosphere/

140 degrees F. This is one reason why they are spraying Sulphur into the atmosphere, so that air temperatures are artificially high.

If you have ever been in a desert area of Arizona or New Mexico, the snakes and lizards get active when the temperatures get very hot – and when the temperatures become cool, they tend to hibernate. This is one reason Area 51 was established north of Reno, Nevada in the desert, and the joint U.S. Military human/Reptilian base was setup at the hot, desert Four Corners area of New Mexico, Colorado, Utah, and Arizona.

The U.S. Navy planes over Moses Lake, Washington also spray large amounts of barium and strontium. These chemicals cause still births and infertility in young couples, which is another attempt to illegally reduce population in the area. In addition, the spraying of aluminum causes the separation of the two frontal lobes in people's brains, causing Alzheimer's disease and dementia. The rates of these diseases in Moses Lake are high. Other problems are chemically induced bronchitis and pneumonia.

If Moses Lake, Washington was a work site covered by the U.S. Department of Labor OSHA regulations, the entire area would have to be immediately evacuated, according to Therese Aigner, an environmental consultant in Pennsylvania. (See Appendix C.)

⌘   ⌘   ⌘

Implants

How can the Reptilians and Greys control humans to make them spray hazardous chemicals which cause the above mentioned diseases? As previously explained, the Reptilians and their slave species do not have any free will – everything is controlled.

Before 1986, the Reptilians and the Greys used metallic implants to control and influence humans on this planet. After 1986, through satellites, they implemented new technology, which infected all humans on this planet with negative implants in the lower Astral plane of the 4th Dimension. The negative implants enable the Greys and the Reptilians to control the population and make people negative. Bill Gates has played a key role in implementing these negative implants worldwide through computers and the satellite system.[2]

As a result of these electro-magnetic implants, many people are now controlled on this planet. These Forth dimensional devices are invisible to the human eye, but act as very real controls on peoples' behavior. The implants are fear based, preventing people from seeking spiritual solutions and answers. Instead, they keep people in a constant state of fear – this feeds and delights the Greys and the Reptilians, since they feed off fear and negativity from this plane.

There are two levels of implants: (a) one is superficial and some people (including myself) have had them removed, and (b) the other implant is attached to one's soul. They can be removed, but only with help from the Galactic Alliance. If you need assistance removing these implants, a very simple technique to use it to say "hu" for 10 or 15 minutes a night.

---

[2] The history of Mr. Gates' collaboration dates from 1996 when he was offered a choice between having his company (Microsoft) broken up, or if he agreed to work with the negative entities, he would be allowed to keep his company. Mr. Gates chose the latter and he has been collaborating with the Reptilians and other negative forces within the U.S. Government ever since. He himself is now controlled.

"Hu" is ancient and comes from the "hu" in "human." Saying "hu" daily will bring you peace and serenity; it will also be a red flag to the Galactics to help you take out these implants. The Galactics will also help people with almost any other situation or problem. (See: "Spiritual protections – the Hu and white light" in Appendix D.)

Most (if not all) of the world's leaders are largely still controlled by these negative implants, and the negative Reptilian influence on the U.S. Government has made Washington D.C. the implant capitol of the world.

Washington D.C. is where leaders such as Prime Minister Abe of Japan and the Prime Minister of Canada, Justen Trudeau, have been implanted while visiting President Obama. The security agents around President Obama are not human, they are Reptilians/Greys who control the President's actions. According to Ambassador Torwellian of the Galactic Alliance, they all have small black boxes around their waste which allow them to control the President.

There is a fascinating You Tube video of one such alien "security agent" around President Obama that was filmed by Israeli Television at an APAC summit meeting in 2012; the video shows a so called "human" security agent for Obama change back and forth from human to Grey/Reptilian alien. If you study pictures of President Obama, you will see this same security agent with President Obama on nearly every trip abroad, anywhere he goes.[3] According to the Galactic Alliance, this entity is controlling President Obama and running the United States. Mr. Obama no longer has any free will.

However, the good news is that Galactic Alliance is quietly working behind the scenes as I write this to neutralize these implants, and give humanity our free will back.

[3]   "Obama's Alien & Reptilian Spotted at AIPAC 2011/2012 – Finding UFO" at https://www.youtube.com/watch?v=ZR7WbCrJEsg

The true nature of humanity is to be kind, benevolent, and loving. Because of this, once these implants are removed, I know people will chose to work with each other to create a beautiful new planet where people live in harmony and peace.

⌘   ⌘   ⌘

Mahatma Gandhi

Contact with the Masters

https://en.wikipedia.org/wiki/File:Gandhi_smiling_R.jpg

As I was receiving messages from the Galactic Alliance, Mahatma Gandhi came to me last year. He said that he wanted me to give a message of nonviolence to humanity. He said that nonviolence for positive social change is especially important, because there is a tremendous change that is happening on this planet.

The change is happening (as Jack Kennedy has noted) from the bottom up. In other words, positive change is coming from humanity itself, from the mass of people of this planet – not from the so called "leaders" of the planet. And as Professor Albert Einstein has said, "We should strive not to use violence in fighting for our cause ... but by non-participation in anything you believe is evil.[1]"

Mahatma Gandhi fought and won independence for India from the British Empire using nonviolence. This is still his profound message today. He says when you fight negativity with negativity you can become as bad as the people you are fighting. To effect positive social change and create a better planet, nonviolence is always the best way.

He wants me to tell humanity that there are wonderful changes coming to this planet. However, we will have to take an active role in creating the beautiful future all of us want for ourselves, our children and our children's children. Siri Gandhi gave me his famous quote that we should all "be the change we want to see." He was able to kick the British out of India in 1947 through nonviolence, even when the British used violence against him and his supporters.

Mr. Gandhi said the water protectors at the Standing Rock Indian Reservation in North Dakota were able to stop the oil pipeline in November 2016 by using nonviolence with thousands and thousands of people standing up to the oil companies and other negative entities. They were successful because there are far

---

[1]   http://www.openculture.com/2013/01/albert_einstein_expresses_his_admiration_for_mahatma_gandhi.html

more light workers on this planet than there are negative entities. Another example he cited was in 1942 during World War II in Denmark. The Nazis wanted all schools to teach Nazi doctrine to children, but every single teacher refused. When everyone stood up to the Nazis, not one teacher went to a concentration camp. There were too many people. It is the same way with anything the negative forces try to impose upon humanity. Mr. Gandhi says that we have strength in numbers. We are all powerful spiritual beings here to do good things on this planet.

⌘   ⌘   ⌘

⌘   ⌘   ⌘

Nostradamus

Contact with the Great Spirits

Image Source: http://Commons.Wikimedia.org

After speaking with Professor Einstein, and his friends J. Robert Oppenheimer, Nikola Tesla, Senator Robert F. Kennedy, Jack Kennedy, President Eisenhower, and Mahatma Gandhi, Professor Einstein then introduced me to Nostradamus, Michel de Nostradame.

When I first contacted Mr. Nostradamus in 2014, he was sitting at his wooden desk, the date was December 1540 in his time line. It was cold outside his home; he had a fire going to keep him warm. The air in his home was smoky and he was sitting there with a quill pen. When I first contacted him, he was rewriting all his quatrains (or passages) which had predicted a Third World War and Armageddon. He said everything changed in March 2011, when Fukushima occurred.

Nostradamus had previously seen a series of conflicts and disasters ahead for humanity, with World War III starting as a conflict in the Balkans in 1993 (the same place where World War I started in 1914). The conflict spread worldwide with a series of nuclear battles waged around the globe headed up by the Anti-Christ. Under this old time line, Nostradamus had seen a series of conflicts and bloodshed, especially in Europe and in the United States. He had previously given the details of all these events under this old time line to the famous American psychic and medium, Deloris Cannon in the late 1980s, in her three-volume set, *Conversations with Nostradamus* published in 1989.

Nostradamus was happy to talk to me, because the time line has changed, because he said there would be no Third World War or Armageddon. Despite the concerted efforts of negative entities to create tragic events, they will not be successful. However, he said that humanity must become more responsible; we must realize we all have an important part to play in co-creating a new bright, beautiful future for this planet!

He said it is well known in Japan that the Fukushima disaster was a "man-made event." Nostradamus said it was done by placing a nuclear bomb at the bottom of the Sea of Japan, so that when the bomb detonated, the resulting Tsunami would destroy all four nuclear reactors at Fukushima. The bomb was planted by an Israeli nuclear submarine.

The Fukushima disaster was to punish Japan for selling enriched plutonium to Iran. The safety systems at all four nuclear reactors were shut off one hour before the Tsunami hit, by an Israeli company under contract to TEPCO (the Tokyo Electric Power Company). This was done so that the reactors would explode, releasing as much radiation as possible into ocean and all over Japan. He said there was an Israeli company under contract to TEPCO (the Tokyo Electric Power Company) in cooperation with a number of negative entities which had engineered the Fukushima disaster. The Reptilians and some negative entities wanted to ultimately reduce the world's population by 95 percent with the deaths from the radiation.

The Galactic Alliance then told me the Reptilians and their slave species (the Greys) had done the same thing in 22 other star systems as they are trying to do here on Earth. They would come to a planet and promise the elite some benefits for cooperating with them. Then they would reduce the planet's population to what they consider is a "manageable" slave like population of about 500 million. The Reptilians would then extract whatever resources they want. When finished, they would destroy the planet completely.

Nostradamus says this will not be allowed to happen here on Earth, since the planet is slated for ascension into the higher dimensions. Furthermore, after the Fukushima disaster in March 2011, I am told the Galactic Alliance was given permission to intervene for the Supreme Being (or God, the entity that created all this) to stop the Reptilians/Greys and their negative human allies.

Dr. Emoto has said humanity on this planet is 80 percent neutral, with 10 percent positive and 10 negative. He said we only needed to change one percent of the people of this planet from either neutral or negative to positive, and the entire planet would change.

In September 2016, the good news is that the entire planet shifted from the negative into the positive, thanks to the efforts of millions of light workers and help from great spirits on the other side, as well as the Galactic Alliance! In addition, from September 5th to 15th, 2016, and then again on September 23rd and 24th, 2016, the entire planet was hit with tremendous positive energy waves, which lifted the planet into the higher dimensions. A second series of positive energy waves hit the planet from December 21st, 2016 to January 7th, 2017. In fact, the Schumann Resonance frequencies hit a high of 90 Hertz (a new record!) on April 16-17, 2017, and then spiked to 120 Hertz, with more positive waves of energy to come![1]

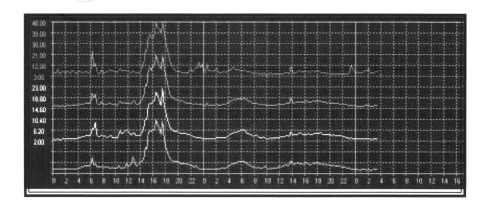

These waves are the start of a series of positive energy waves, which will eventually help propel and shift this entire planet into the higher dimensions! Dr. Emoto says we are now on our way!

---

[1]   Data from the "Space Monitoring Station" in Tomsk, Russia. Link: http://sosrff. tsu.ru/?page_id=12
and http://whispersfromthesoul.com/2017/05/schumann-resonance-spikes-may-8th-110-120-hertz/

Ascension/Energy Waves

Contact with the Great Spirits

The Earth is slated for ascension, and the ascension process has already begun, with powerful positive energy waves hitting the planet right now. This is the first time in at least 25,800 years (which represents the Mayan time cycle) that the Earth has changed from the negative into the positive. In fact, according to UFO expert researcher Alfred Lambremont Webre, this is the first time in THREE Mayan 25,800 year cycles (or 77,400 years) the planet has changed from the negative into the positive.[1]

In addition to these energy waves hitting the planet, this positive change in the planet is coming from the bottom up (in other words, from people like you and me) — not from the top down (i.e., from Governments or large corporations). So all of us can now play a real part in making this world a better and happier place! According to Jack Kennedy, we are NOT "powerless" — all of us are POWERFUL spiritual beings and we are here to create a beautiful planet!

Although Fukushima was a tragic event, the really positive thing that happened is after it occurred, both the Supreme Being (or God) and the Galactic Alliance stepped in. As a result, the time line has now completely changed and there will now be absolutely no Armageddon or Third World War. According to Nostradamus, all the previous predictions of doom and gloom have now completely changed; there will be no world ending event. But we each have a part to play in creating this future, it will not just be handed to us. Since we are all co-creators with the Supreme Being we will have to work at creating this new future together. The good news is we are getting real help!

For example, in November 2016, my Galactic friends tell me the cabal or negative entities tried to cause another meltdown at Fukushima with another so called "earthquake" in the Sea of Japan at the same exact location where a nuclear

---

[1]   www.outofthisworld1150.com/guests/alfred-lambremont-webre-med-jd/

bomb was detonated by an Israeli submarine in March 2011. Although this caused a 7.4 "earthquake," and the government was concerned about another Tsunami, the Galactics neutralized the effect of the bomb, and there was no disaster at Fukushima, even though (once again) some of the safety systems were either turned off, or conveniently did not work.[2]

The negative entities are trying to destroy humanity and planet Earth. However, they will ultimately fail in their efforts. This is because we are now getting help, and we are being protected.

In my conversations with Nostradamus, he says the time line for humanity has now changed from destruction, to a bright future. I welcome this change, as it means good news for all of here on planet Earth, and we can use some good news! Nostradamus says that we are powerful spiritual beings, destined to create a beautiful and harmonious planet where everyone lives in peace. We have a bright and wonderful future ahead of us!

According to Nostradamus, time is like a flowing river which, depending on one's choices can flow any number of ways. I can see Nostradamus is now sitting at his desk, crossing out all his previous quatrains, in which he had predicted World War III, and doom and gloom. He has taken out his quill pen, and made broad black strokes through the old quatrains, and is now sitting in front of blank parchment, ready to write. He is asking, "What kind of future will you help him write? Will you help create a new happy future for humanity, based on harmony, love, and gratitude? Or will you continue to perpetuate the old ways of doing things, where people fight and live in negativity and disharmony? I hope you will all choose the former to help create

[2]   "Probe of Fukushima Daini's Nº3 Reactor Cooling System Knocked Offline After Earthquake", https://nuclear-news.net/2016/11/24/probe-of-fukushima-dainis-n3-reactor-cooling-system-knocked-offline-after-earthquake/ , and "Japan earthquake: tsunami warning lifted after 7.4 magnitude quake – as it happened", at: https://www.theguardian.com/world/live/2016/nov/21/japan-earthquake-tsunami-warning-live-updates

a bright new future for this planet and the people of Earth!"

When Professor Einstein wrote his "Bomb of Love" letter to his daughter in 1955, he wrote that "Love is God and God is Love" — he tells me that he would have never helped create the atomic bomb if he had to do everything over again. This is very profound and important, because this is the same message that was given to President Dwight D. Eisenhower when he met with the Pleiadians and the Galactic Alliance in 1953! This is also the same message that Dr. Emoto has for humanity. Love and gratitude are the most important and powerful forces on this planet, which can and will help transform this Earth into the place where we may live in peace and harmony!

⌘   ⌘   ⌘

Zorra and the People of Hollow Earth

Contact with the Great Spirits

Original art by Stephanie Cardinal, repirnted with permission

We have been at these crossroads before, where we could chose the high road and become a beautiful, benevolent planet based on love and harmony. Or we could chose a lower road, and destroy ourselves with the ugliness of hate, war, and conflict. Approximately 12,500 years ago, we were at one such crossroads when the military elite faction of Atlantis gained control over their unique, advanced civilization and started a nuclear war, which ended up destroying all of Atlantis and Lemuria. Many of the same souls who were present then are back again now, trying to change things in a positive way to rectify the mistakes of the past.

Professor Einstein, Nickola Telsa, and Dr. Emoto were all present during the destruction of Atlantis 12,500 years ago. I was also present as a priest in one of the temples of Atlantis; we all tried to stop the madness back then. Unfortunately, we failed then, but we will be successful now, because the tide has turned, and we are getting needed help.

When Lemuria was destroyed by the Atlanteans thousands of years ago, only 25,000 people from Lemuria were able to escape to the safety of the hollow earth, beneath Mt. Shasta in northern California.[1] Fortunately, they were able to bring all of their technology with them; their population now numbers about 1.3 million. The Lemurians under Mt. Shasta are very advanced, loving beings. They are now coming out to help us here on the surface, so that we do not destroy ourselves, since what happens here on the surface of this planet directly affects them.

For example, after Fukushima released massive amounts of radiation into the atmosphere, some of that radiation

---

[1]   I lead a tour to Mt. Shasta and the Hollow Earth every year – if you are interested in coming along, please email me at outofthisworld1150@gmail.com. During my tour to Shasta in 2016, six people from Korea actually went into Telos and Shambala. There is a lot of spiritual preparation for such a trip, including meditation. They had meditated for over three years, before they were allowed to come into the Hollow Earth for a visit. I am not saying that you will need to meditate for three years to visit Telos, but it does help to meditate to prepare for the trip.

went into the Hollow Earth, since they obtain their air from our surface atmosphere. Thus, it is in their interest (as well as ours) for them to clean up Fukushima

One such entity who I have been in contact with since early 2016 has been Zorra of the Hollow Earth, a wonderful, benevolent Lemurian who cares deeply about us here on the surface of planet Earth. Channeled by his son, Billie Woodard, Zorra has been on my radio and television program several times; you can listen to him at: www.OutOfThisWorld1150.com

One of the most important things he has said is that we have the spark of the Supreme Being (or God) within all of us. We can ask the Supreme Being to help us with anything. As one example, Zorra and Billie gave me this special healing prayer to share with you.

If you have any physical or spiritual problem or issue you would like help with, please say this prayer and it should help you: "Five, four, three, two, one, I receive from God (if you are man) or Goddess (if you are a woman), help and healing for _____ (list the help that you need), and I know it to be true."

Please say this prayer as many times as you like — I have tried this myself, and it really does work! Zorra also gave me his picture, and he said that it was infused with healing love and light (see the beginning of Chapter 15). If you meditate on his picture, or place it on whatever part of your body that needs healing, it will really help!

Zorra has green skin, because his blood is copper based, but is human just like us!

We are receiving intergalactic and spiritual help in a way we have never received before from the Supreme Being who created the universe. We are also receiving help from the Galactic Alliance, many ascended Masters, and other loving, benevolent spiritual beings. The Galactics and the people of the Hollow Earth have stepped in and are continually cleaning up Fukushima, so we are not poisoned by the radiation. In fact, during the cold war between the USSR and the US, the Galactics stepped in and shut down the U.S. and Russian nuclear missiles at least 8 different times, so we would not destroy ourselves. .

⌘   ⌘   ⌘

The New Earth

Contact with the Great Spirits

We are building the New Earth based on harmony and cooperation, rather than on conflict and war, with service to others, rather than on "service to self." Jack Kennedy says the old Earth is one where there is competition, disharmony and war. "Service to self" is based on negativity, selfishness, and hate. The new Earth is one where there will be: cooperation, harmony, peace, and service to others based on love. Those of the lower vibration will feel trapped, it will be the same old, same old for them. If they don't change, they will move to a lower vibrational Earth that has been set aside for them. They will not realize that the world has changed.

However, those who raise their vibrations will eventually become light bodies, filled with high vibrations from the Prime Creator, or the Supreme Being. We also need to take care of this planet in a much better way than in the past. Part of the problem is the influence of the Reptilians. They are a resource driven species who look to exploit planets like Earth, and do not care if they destroy life in the process. Consider the destruction of human civilization during Atlantean times 12,500 years ago. Mother Earth can and will fight back; we need her a lot more than she needs us. The Earth is a living entity. The current floods like the one in West Virginia, are a mechanism where by Mother Earth can cleanse herself of the pollution caused by all the fracking and mining. The oil fracking in this country is a deliberate attempt to sever the connections between the people of this planet and Mother Earth, by polluting and destroying the water, the life blood of the planet.

We have reached the tipping point, and this year (2017) and next (2018) will be a pivotal years in humanity's future. What we do this year and next will determine our future for many hundreds, even thousands, of years to come! The true nature of humanity is to be kind, loving, and benevolent. I know that we will make the right choices to create a bright, harmonious planet.

I have been asked by Professor Albert Einstein, Nostradamus, J. Robert Oppenheimer, Leonardo da Vinci, U.S. President John F. Kennedy, Senator Robert F. Kennedy, Dr. Masaru Emoto, Mahatma Gandhi, Nicola Tesla, U.S. President Dwight D. Eisenhower and Galactic Alliance to write this book to let people know that we have a very bright and enlightened future ahead of all of us! However, they also say that we together need to make the right choices so that this future will materialize, not only for ourselves, but also our children and for future generations.

The purpose of this book is (a) to raise consciousness, (b) make this world a far better and much happier place, and (c) to inspire people to make the right choices to create this better world. This can be done in many ways, but one of the most important ways is to start by treating the planet and your fellow humans with as much love, kindness, and respect as possible. The changes that are happening now are coming from the bottom up, from the people like you and me who are changing the world to make it a better and happier place! Because of the world wide controls placed on many world leaders, I would not look for any help from the governments of the world. Instead, we should focus on what we can do for our planet and all who live on it, one person at a time. People like you and I can make this world a better place.

Jack Kennedy stated that these changes would have happened in the early 1960s when he was President, but since it our destiny to create a loving, benevolent planet, these positive changes are coming now, and they are coming very fast.

This is also a time of truth, where things which are false will fall by the wayside and those things which are true will become even more self-evident. It is part of our natural evolution into the 5th Dimension. There is only truth in the 5th and higher Dimensions.

In the 16th Century, Nostradamus predicted that by the 2020s or 2030s, that humanity on this planet would enter into a 1000 years of peace and spiritual prosperity, resulting in a true "golden age" for humanity... Wars and poverty would become a thing of the past, and after this 1000 year period was over, we would then become a space faring species (much like on Star Trek).

I totally agree with Nostradamus in his predictions, and I know that our future is very, very bright! I am not a "doom and gloomer," and I don't think we can afford to think negatively about our future!

With these very positive changes, the dream of both President Eisenhower and President Kennedy in creating a much better and happier planet will be realized. As President Eisenhower stated in his famous "Secret Societies" speech:[1]

"We pray that peoples of all faiths, all races, all nations, may have their great human needs satisfied; that those now denied opportunity shall come to enjoy it to the full; that all who yearn for freedom may experience its spiritual blessings; that those who have freedom will understand, also, its heavy responsibilities; that all who are insensitive to the needs of others will learn charity; that the scourges of poverty, disease and ignorance will be made to disappear from the earth, and that, in the goodness of time, all peoples will come to live together in a peace guaranteed by the binding force of mutual respect and love."

Dr. Emoto admired and respected Professor Einstein and now that they are on the other side, they are great friends, and are working together to help humanity progress and spiritually evolve. They both want me to note that love is the most powerful and important force in the universe.

As Professor Einstein wrote in his famous letter, "A Bomb of

---

[1]   http://whowhatwhy.org/2016/01/17/he-told-us-so-president-eisenhowers-military-industrial-complex-speech/

Love" to his daughter,[2]

"*There is an extremely powerful force that, so far, science has not found a formal explanation to. It is a force that includes and governs all others, and is even behind any phenomenon operating in the universe and has not yet been identified by us.*

This universal force is LOVE.

When scientists looked for a unified theory of the universe they forgot the most powerful unseen force.

Love is Light, that enlightens those who give and receive it.

Love is gravity, because it makes some people feel attracted to others.

Love is power, because it multiplies the best we have, and allows humanity not to be extinguished in their blind selfishness.

Love unfolds and reveals.

For love we live and die.

Love is God and God is Love.

This force explains everything and gives meaning to life. This is the variable that we have ignored for too long, maybe because we are afraid of love because it is the only energy in the universe that man has not learned to drive at will."

[2]   https://suedreamwalker.wordpress.com/2015/04/15/a-letter-from-albert-einstein-to-his-daughter-about-the-universal-force-which-is-love/

Dr. Emoto found that "Love and Gratitude" produced the most beautiful crystal he ever photographed:[3]

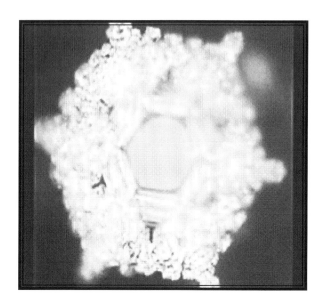

When Dr. Emoto discovered the power of love, he gave a speech before the United Nations in 2005, in which he started what he called his "Emoto Peace Project," where he would distribute books on the message of love and gratitude to children all over the world — see: www.emotoevents.com/events.

Since then, he and Michiko Hayashi (who is now the Global Director and Ambassador of the Emoto Peace Project), have distributed hundreds of thousands of copies of his beautiful *Messages from Water* (Children's book) to children around the world.

It has been translated into over 25 different languages and distributed to children in those countries — see: http://www.emotoevents.com/events/. The goal of the program is to teach children the value of love and gratitude, so that as adults, they will want to create a world based upon harmony and peace,

---

[3]   Water Crystal photograph Copyright 2017 Office Masaru Emoto LLC

rather than fighting and war. See: www.emotopeaceproject.me. The Emoto Peace Project is a wonderful endeavor that is creating a much better and happier world, by teaching children the value of love and gratitude

As Nikola Tesla says:

"Life is a rhythm that must be comprehended. I feel the rhythm and direct on it and pamper in it. It was very grateful and gave me the knowledge I have. Everything that lives is related to a deep and wonderful relationship: man and the stars, amoebas' and the sun, the heart and the circulation of an infinite number of worlds. These ties are unbreakable, but they can be tame and to propitiate and begin to create new and different relationships in the world, and that does not violate the old.

Knowledge comes from space; our vision is its most perfect set. We have two eyes: the earthly and spiritual. It is recommended that it become one eye. Universe is alive in all its manifestations, like a thinking animal. Stone is a thinking and sentient being, such as plant, beast and a man. A star that shines asked to look at, and if we are not a sizeable self-absorbed we would understand its language and message. His breathing, his eyes and ears of the man must comply with breathing, eyes and ears of the Universe."[4]

Mr. Tesla said, "The entire Universe is in certain periods sick of itself, and of us, because we have treated this Earth very poorly." But he said, "That we must learn these truths in order to be healed. "The remedy is in our hearts and — in the heart of the animals that we call the Universe."[5]

In other words, we need to look within our hearts to find

---

[4]   http://sciencevibe.com/2017/04/05/teslas-sad-last-interview-im-a-defeated-man-i-wanted-to-illuminate-the-whole-earth/

[5]   http://sciencevibe.com/2017/04/05/teslas-sad-last-interview-im-a-defeated-man-i-wanted-to-illuminate-the-whole-earth/

the answers to heal not only ourselves, but the planet and the universe.   And as part of this, he tells me that we are all one – we are all part of this beautiful universe.

⌘   ⌘   ⌘

Conclusion

The Golden Age

All the great spirits say we are all powerful spiritual beings. They all say that it is our destiny to make this planet a truly beautiful place where people and the Earth and all living things live in harmony and peace. The Prime Creator has slated the Earth for ascension into the 5th and higher dimensions, and nothing can stop that; however, because we are all co-creators with the Supreme Being, we have a responsibility to take care of God's creation, and help in this evolutionary spiritual process.

Jack Kennedy would have started this process over 50 year ago if he had not been killed; he says that it is our destiny to create a beautiful, peaceful planet, and that history is repeating itself now with these positive changes.

Jack Kennedy wants to tell everyone reading this book that the old Earth was based on competition, disharmony, war, service to self, negativity and hate. The new Earth will be based on cooperation, harmony, peace, service to others, positivity and love. We must all play a part in this new Earth. In the words of Jack's famous "Ask Not" speech of 1961, he says again, "And so my fellow Americans, ask not what your country can do for you, ask what you can do for your country ... My fellow citizens of the world, ask not what America will do for you, but what together we can do for the freedom of mankind." Jack says these words are even more important today, and he would only change what he said in 1961 to: "My fellow citizens of the world ask not what America will do for you, but what together we can do for the freedom of all peoples to create a beautiful, peaceful planet."

Jack Kennedy was a true visionary and his words are as important today as they were in 1961. I am certain that if we all work together, we can and will create a much better and happier planet! Our future is very, very bright for ourselves, our children and for future generations!

To create this beautiful new world, Professor Einstein has said, "We are concerned not merely with the technical problem of securing and maintaining peace, but also the important tasks of education and enlightenment."

Freedom is essential for this beautiful new world, because as Professor Einstein has said, "Without such freedom, there would have no Shakespeare, no Goethe, no Newton, no Faraday, no Pasteur, and no Lister."

Although Professor Einstein says that "Science has provided the possibility for human beings from the possibility of hard labor, — when the ideas are war and conquest, those tools become as dangerous as razors in the hands of a child of three." He said, "We must not condemn man's inventiveness and patient conquest of the forces of nature because they are being used wrongly," but "the fate of humanity is entirely dependent upon its moral development."[1]

I hope everyone reading this book will join me, and all my friends (Professor Albert Einstein, Nostradamus, J. Robert Oppenheimer, Leonardo da Vinci, U.S. President John F. Kennedy, Senator Robert F. Kennedy, Dr. Masaru Emoto, Mahatma Gandhi, Nicolay Tesla, U.S. President Dwight D. Eisenhower, and Galactic Alliance) in creating this new, beautiful golden age!

⌘　⌘　⌘

---

[1] https://www.facebook.com/curiositydotcom/videos/1630971483597329/

⌘   ⌘   ⌘

Appendix A

Contacting the Spirit World and
Proof of the Other Side

We all have psychic abilities, and with proper training, we can all communicate with the other side. Spirits who have passed on, communicate through thoughts from the higher dimensions, so when you want to talk to either a relative or friend who has passed on, all you need do is just meditate, sit quietly and send love and light to the one that you want communicate with. Love is the most powerful force in the universe — it is also the currency of the higher dimensions.

Spirits from the other side in other dimensions are always around us. They show themselves in various ways. I have found one of the easiest ways for them to show themselves is to come through in photographs, like in the picture at the beginning of Appendix A.

In this picture, there is a red orb in the lower right hand corner, and surrounding the sun are also multiple lighter reddish orbs. Each orb represents a spirit, and since they are light bodies, it is sometimes easiest for them to come through photographs. Much of what you see in this picture is what I call "angel light," or the streaks of light from the sun. This is not just an optical illusion; it is actually angelic light from the 5th and higher dimensions where spirits live.

When I was flying from Vancouver, Canada to Tokyo in April 2016, in the middle of the night 39,000 feet above the Pacific Ocean, I was given the message to photograph the moon. It was a beautiful moonlit night. When I took the picture on the following page, a beautiful angel appeared.

On the original picture, pink appeared at each end of the angel's image, which represents love.

Picture of angel on flight from Vancouver to Tokyo © Ted Mahr.

As a psychic, my accuracy rate is very high. Sometimes I am contacted by spirits who want to convey advice and messages to their family and friends. I have been doing this for over 20 years. It is now just as easy for me to talk to a spirit in the 5th Dimension as it is to talk to someone in this 3rd Dimensional physical reality.

In this lifetime, my spiritual journey started in February 1978 when I was almost killed in a 110 mph head on car accident with a drunk driver. I was driving a Volkswagen Beetle; the other driver was driving a Pontiac Bonneville. When he hit me head on, my head hit the steering wheel and shattered my jaw and damaged my hearing. I could have easily died, but I know now that it was not my time yet to pass over. Later, I learned that each of us has contracted to spend so many years here on Earth, and my contract is for 87 years. I am now 62, so I have 25 more years left on my contract to evolve and accomplish my soul purpose.

A few months after my accident, I was recuperating at my parent's farm on the outskirts of Olympia, Washington when I walked back into their 10 acre woods of beautiful, timeless pine trees and saw the sun coming through the mists of a morning spring rain. When I looked up at the sparkling bright sun that morning, I realized I did not die in that car accident, because I had many things still to accomplish.

My foster mother (Teri) was a Master Psychic. In 1994, she started giving me readings. I will never forget the first time that I walked into her living room and she gave me a reading. As I walked into her house, she read everything on my mind with 100 percent accuracy, and then gave me all the answers to my questions, before I could ask them! From that time in 1994 until her passing in 2012, she taught me how to contact the other side. With her help, the spirits gave me many, many tests to make sure I was receiving their messages correctly. I am so grateful to her (and my wonderful spirit family) for helping me in so many ways!

When my father passed away in March 1999, he contacted

Teri. With his help, he has given me spiritual guidance, and constant life reviews. Normally, you only receive a "life review" when you pass over. In a life review, you review all your thoughts, actions, and deeds – not only from your perspective, but also from the perspective of every one you have interacted with, including animals. Thanks to the help of both my Dad and Teri, I have been given constant and multiple life reviews every day since 1994, or for the last 23 years.

According to my spirit family, I have advanced over 300 spiritual lifetimes, thanks so their help. If each spiritual lifetime is 80 Earth years, I have advanced over 24,000 years. As a result, I am now able to see into the past, present and future. I also read minds and see auras. It is as easy for me to talk to someone in this Third Dimension as to talk to someone who has passed on to the Fifth or higher dimensions like President Kennedy and other great spirits. I can telepathically talk to Ambassador Torwellian of the Galactic Alliance, or Zorra of the Hollow Earth.

I think everyone has the ability to talk to the other side, but people sometimes don't have the confidence to develop these abilities. I was very lucky to have my wonderful foster mother Teri who helped me develop my psychic abilities. Teri was a master psychic who helped police departments in the Seattle, Washington USA area find lost and missing children and she was very good at what she did. However, she told me it was depressing work because sometimes she would help locate children who had been murdered or abused.

The main way spirits on the other side communicate is through thought. The physical structures of the 5th Dimension are just as real as that of this 3rd Dimension, but different in the sense that when spirits communicate with us in this 3rd Dimension, they use thought as the main way to communicate. They may also communicate through animals, clouds, and other objects as well. Another way a spirit can communicate is to materialize a penny— I call a "penny from heaven" — usually face up

(Abraham Lincoln's face upward) in front of you. I have had this happen many, many times. For example, sometimes when I am driving long distances, I will stop at a rest stop, and when I return to my car, a "penny from heaven" will appear on the ground, right in front of the door to my car. This is the spirits' way to let you know that they are with you, and helping protect you.

Other ways spirits communicate is through light, especially during sunsets where orbs of light will appear. The easiest way to see these orbs is to simply take a photograph, and you will see the orbs appearing in the light. I've done this many, many times, and since each spirit has a particular color (which depends on their sole purpose and spiritual development), I can always tell who is with me. My wonderful and loving father, for example, is a reddish color, and my brother, Robert, is a blue orb. On the other hand, my sister, Lisa, is a greenish/yellow color, and Aunt Sophie is a pure white color. Red can be a very powerful color. Blue indicates that the spirit is interested in its sole purpose.

The color of my aura is blue because I am interested in my soul purpose. White is the perfect color, closest to God (the Prime Creator); yellow is a happy color and green is for healing. If you are a doctor or nurse, the color of your soul would likely be green since this is the color for healing.

Each of us has at least one guardian Angel around us. They help protect us, provide spiritual guidance and moral support whenever you need it. So whenever you deserted or need guidance on any subject, please know that you are never alone – your guides are always around you.

There are 12 different dimensions. We exist in the 3rd Dimension, and Angels typically exist in the 5th Dimension or higher. Thoughts are tangible things in the 5th Dimension, and take precedence over things in the 3rd Dimension, so it is very important to keep your thoughts as positive as possible. Your thoughts directly affect what happens in your 3rd Dimensional world.

There is no thing such as "death." When you pass over, you simply make a transition to a higher and lighter dimension and trade your old body for a new model. Time as we know it exists in the 3rd and 4th Dimensions. Time does not exist in the 5th Dimension, thus there is no past, present, or future, everything just "exists." This allows a good psychic who can go into the 5th Dimension, to see into the future with great accuracy. Good psychics can do what is called "remote viewing" and see past, present or future with great accuracy.

Occasionally, you will also see spirits in the corner of your eye. Because spirits exist in fifth and higher dimensions, they make their presence known through your peripheral vision. Spirits are usually vibrating at a higher frequency than in this 3rd Dimension so the easiest way for them to communicate with us is through thought. Often, when you want to communicate with for example a loved one on the other side, the easiest way to just to send them a thought or a question like, "how are you?" And they will answer immediately. The FIRST response you receive is most often the answer from them.

Other times, spirits may use an animal (like a bird or even a butterfly) to communicate with you. For example, let's say you are thinking of your wonderful Grandmother who passed on years ago. Suddenly, a bird comes to your window and stays there looking at you for hours. That is probably your Grandmother telling you that she is with you and that she loves you!!

Another way spirits can communicate is to give you scent of their favorite perfume or cologne. There have been times when I have smelled the scent of my Dad when he used to work out in the woods behind our farmhouse where I grew up. Whenever I would smell his "woodsy scent." I know he was with me, protecting and helping me!

Often when I am driving, I have several beams of what I call "angelic light" come through my window and surround my car completely! It is not sunlight; it is angelic light and when it happens, I always am so blessed because I know that I am loved and protected! (See attached picture of angelic light coming through my front car window)

Footnote: For those interested, communicating with spirits is very easy to do, once you learn how. If you are interested in learning how to communicate with the other side, please email me at outofthisworld1150@gmail.com.   I will be glad to teach you how I do it.

Appendix B

Radiation Water Tests Off Seattle and Pacific Ocean—No Radiation from Fukushima

In March 2014, I had the water of the Pacific Ocean tested off of Ocean Shores, Washington, just north of Aberdeen, Washington. The water was tested for radiation from Fukushima.

As noted by radiation expert Arnie Gundersen in an email to me dated April 4, 2014, the radioactive potasium (K-40) was occurring from the atomic bomb tests of the 1950s and 1960s. However, the radiation from Fukushima mostly consisted of radioactive Cesium 134 and 137 (Cs 134 and Cs 137). Significantly, no Cs 134 nor Cs 137 were found in the water sample.

Copies of the test results are included on the following pages.

Wisconsin State Laboratory of Hygiene
2601 Agriculture Drive, PO Box 7996
Madison, WI 53707-7996
(800)442-4618 • FAX (608)224-6213
http://www.slh.wisc.edu

Laboratory Report

D.F. Kurtycz, M.D., Medical Director • Charles D. Brokopp, Dr.P.H., Director

Environmental Health Division		Radiochemistry	

WDNR LAB ID: 113133790   NELAP LAB ID: E37658   EPA LAB ID: WI00007   WI DATCP ID: 105-415

Supplement to test report#:   9568413

WSLH Sample: RY001430   **Provisional Report**

TED MAHR   Bill To

                                                      Customer ID: 346414
                                                      TED MAHR

Collection Date: 03/08/2014 13:00:00   Collected By: T MAHR
Owner: Well Completion Date:
Unique Well #:   Account: PP009
Well Construction: Date Received: 03/11/2014 07:24:00
County: Date Reported:
Driller or Pump Installers License #.   TED MAHR   Sample Reason: GRAB SAMPLE
Sampling Location:
Sampling Point: PUBLIC DRINKING ENTRY POINT
Sampling information: SALT WATER
Lat Deg: Min: Long Deg: Min: Method:
Driller:

Analyses and Results:

Analysis Date 03/14/2014 08:41:05	Lab Comment		
Analysis Method	Result	Units	LOD
EPA_901.1 BE-7 ACTIVITY	0.000±0.000	BQ/L	0.297
EPA_901.1 K-40 ACTIVITY	9.56±1.68	BQ/L	1.47
EPA_901.1 MN-54 ACTIVITY	0.000±0.000	BQ/L	0.0386
EPA_901.1 CO-58 ACTIVITY	0.000±0.000	BQ/L	0.0312
EPA_901.1 FE-59 ACTIVITY	0.000±0.000	BQ/L	0.0592
EPA_901.1 CO-60 ACTIVITY	0.000±0.000	BQ/L	0.0420
EPA_901.1 ZN-65 ACTIVITY	0.000±0.000	BQ/L	0.0594
EPA_901.1 NB-95 ACTIVITY	0.000±0.000	BQ/L	0.0354
EPA_901.1 ZR-95 ACTIVITY	0.000±0.000	BQ/L	0.0577
EPA_901.1 RU-103 ACTIVITY	0.000±0.000	BQ/L	0.0359
EPA_901.1 RU-106 ACTIVITY	0.000±0.000	BQ/L	0.277
EPA_901.1 I-131 ACTIVITY	0.000±0.000	BQ/L	0.0313
EPA_901.1 CS-134 ACTIVITY	0.000±0.000	BQ/L	0.0305

Page 1 of 2

Analysis of Water from Pacific Ocean off Ocean Shores, WA taken March 2014. No radiation found except for K-40.

Wisconsin State Laboratory of Hygiene
2601 Agriculture Drive, PO Box 7996
Madison, WI 53707-7996
(800)442-4618 • FAX (608)224-6213
http://www.slh.wisc.edu

Laboratory Report

D.F. Kartyca, M.D., Medical Director • Charles D. Brokopp, Dr.P.H., Director

Environmental Health Division   Radiochemistry

WDNR LAB ID: 113133790   NELAP LAB ID: E37658   EPA LAB ID: WI00007   WI DATCP ID: 105-415

Supplement to test report#:   9568413

WSLH Sample: RY001430   Provisional Report

EPA_901.1 CS-137 ACTIVITY	0.000±0.000	BQ/L	0.0422
EPA_901.1 BA-140 ACTIVITY	0.000±0.000	BQ/L	0.174
EPA_901.1 LA-140 ACTIVITY	0.000±0.000	BQ/L	0.0492
EPA_901.1 CE-141 ACTIVITY	0.000±0.000	BQ/L	0.0754
EPA_901.1 CE-144 ACTIVITY	0.000±0.000	BQ/L	0.279

Test results for NELAP accredited tests are certified to meet the requirements of the NELAC standards. For a list of accredited analytes see http://www.slh.wisc.edu/nelap/

List of Abbreviations:

LOD = Level of detection

Responsible Party: *David Webb*   David Webb, ESS Director

If there are questions about this report, please contact the Radiochemistry Unit at 608-224-6227.

The results in this report apply only to the sample specifically listed above. This report is not to be reproduced except in full.

Report #:   9568415   Page 2 of 2

WSLH

Wisconsin State
Laboratory of Hygiene
http://www.slh.wisc.edu/slh
Environmental Health Division
2601 Agriculture Drive
P.O. Box 7996
Madison, WI 53707-7996
(608)224-6202 (800)442-4618

RADIOACTIVITY IN WATER TEST REQUEST FORM

Please type or print clearly, and be sure that all spaces are filled in. Your test can not be processed unless complete information is provided. There is a cost for each test.

☒ Gamma Scan   ☐ Radium 228   ☐ Tritium
☐ Gross Alpha & Beta ☐ Radium 226 & 228   ☐ Uranium Isotopic
☐ Radium 226   ☐ Strontium 90   ☐ Uranium Total
☐ Radium 224   ☐ Thorium Isotopic   ☐
   Needs to be scheduled

Report to:
(Please print clearly or use your address label)

Name: TED MAHR
PO Box:
Address
City: M
State:
Phone:
Fax:

Customer ID : 346414

Bill to: (if different from Report address)
(Please print clearly or use your address label)

Name:
(Company, Water System):
Address:
City:
State: _____ Zip:
Phone: ( )
Fax: ( )

Sample Description:

Salt water

Well Information:
Complete this section ONLY if you have a well
Unique Well # _____   Example : AB123
PWSID # _____

Collection:
Date: 03/08/14   0945 AM
Time: 13:00 AM or (PM) (circle one)
Collected By: 1300 EST / GOK 070314
County:
Professional License #:

Address Sampled: ☐ (Check if same as **Report** name and address)
Address:
City:
State: _____ Zip:

US Mail Address:
State Lab of Hygiene
Radiochemistry Unit
PO BOX 7996
Madison, WI 53707-7996

UPS/Federal ExpressAddress:
State Lab of Hygiene
Radiochemistry Unit
2601 Agriculture Dr
Madison, WI 53718-6780

PP009

03/11/14
07:24
RY001430

REC'D 1 9.46ℓ CONTAINER
LAB ACIDIFIED AFTER POUR OFF 1ℓ JGB PHL2 031114
2.0mℓ HNO₂   031114

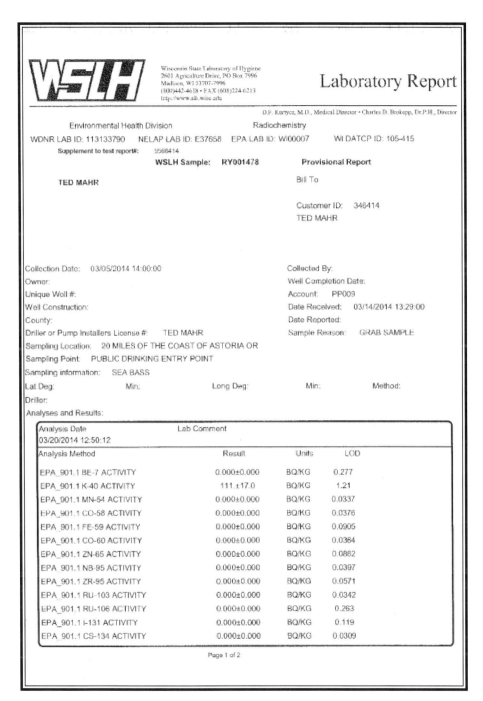

Analysis of Sea Bass—No radiation found, except for K-40.

Wisconsin State Laboratory of Hygiene
2601 Agriculture Drive, PO Box 7996
Madison, WI 53707-7996
(800)442-4618 · FAX (608)224-6213
http://www.slh.wisc.edu

Laboratory Report

D.F. Kartyca, M.D., Medical Director · Charles D. Brokopp, Dr.P.H., Director

Environmental Health Division   Radiochemistry

WDNR LAB ID: 113133790   NELAP LAB ID: E37658   EPA LAB ID: WI00007   WI DATCP ID: 105-415

Supplement to test report#:   9568414

WSLH Sample: RY001478   Provisional Report

EPA_901.1 CS-137 ACTIVITY	0.000±0.000	BQ/KG	0.0738
EPA_901.1 BA-140 ACTIVITY	0.000±0.000	BQ/KG	0.252
EPA_901.1 LA-140 ACTIVITY	0.000±0.000	BQ/KG	0.0704
EPA_901.1 CE-141 ACTIVITY	0.000±0.000	BQ/KG	0.0611
EPA_901.1 CE-144 ACTIVITY	0.000±0.000	BQ/KG	0.191

Test results for NELAP accredited tests are certified to meet the requirements of the NELAC standards. For a list of accredited analytes see
http://www.slh.wisc.edu/nelap/

List of Abbreviations:

LOD = Level of detection

Responsible Party: _David Webb_ David Webb, ESS Director

If there are questions about this report, please contact the Radiochemistry Unit at 608-224-6227.

The results in this report apply only to the sample specifically listed above. This report is not to be reproduced except in full.

Report #:   9568416   Page 2 of 2

RADIOACTIVITY IN WATER TEST REQUEST FORM

WSLH

Wisconsin State Laboratory of Hygiene
http://www.slh.wisc.edu/ehd
Environmental Health Division
2601 Agriculture Drive
P.O. Box 7996
Madison, WI 53707-7996
(608)224-6202 (800)442-4618

Please type or print clearly, and be sure that all spaces are filled in. Your test can not be processed unless complete information is provided. There is a cost for each test.

- ☒ Gamma Scan
- ☐ Gross Alpha & Beta
- ☐ Radium 226
- ☐ Radium 224 *Needs to be scheduled*
- ☐ Radium 228
- ☐ Radium 226 & 228
- ☐ Strontium 90
- ☐ Thorium Isotopic
- ☐ Tritium
- ☐ Uranium Isotopic
- ☐ Uranium Total
- ☐

Report to:
(*Please print clearly or use your address label*)

Name: TED MAHR

PO Box:

Address:

City: M

State:

Phone:

Fax:

Customer ID : 346414
Email: outofthisworld1150@gmail.com

Bill to: (if different from Report address)
(*Please print clearly or use your address label*)

Name:

(Company, Water System):

Address:

City:

State: _____ Zip:

Phone: ( )

Fax: ( )

Sample Description:

SEA BASS

Well Information:
Complete this section ONLY if you have a well

Unique Well # _____ Example : AB123

PWSID # _____

Collection:

Date: 03 / 05 / 14

Time: 12 : 00 AM or (PM) (circle one) PST 14:00 cDT 3/12/14

Collected By:

County:

Professional License #:

Address Sampled: ☐ (Check if same as Report name and address)

Address: 20 MILES OFF THE COAST OF ASTORIA, OR.

City:

State: _____ Zip:

JGB   031714

US Mail Address:
State Lab of Hygiene
Radiochemistry Unit
PO BOX 7996
Madison, WI 53707-7996

UPS/Federal Express Address:
State Lab of Hygiene
Radiochemistry Unit
2601 Agriculture Dr
Madison, WI 53718-6780

PP009

03/14/14
13:29

RY001478

R999 GRN

⌘   ⌘   ⌘

Appendix C

Chem Trail Tests
in Moses Lake, Washington

At the north end of Moses Lake, there is an old U.S. Air Force base that was called "Larsen Air Force Base." Officially it was closed down in 1966, but the military still uses it for chem trail spraying, since runway of this base is the second longest in North America. Located next to the northern part of the runway is a building owned by "Chemi Con." Based in Japan, Chemi Con specializes in heavy metals, and it is "North America's largest supplier of aluminum electrolytic capacitors ...." Its parent company is "Nippon Chemi Con" – see: http://www.chemi-con.com/.

The aluminum and other heavy metals sprayed by the U.S. Navy planes at close range over Moses Lake may come from this company located on the runway in Moses Lake. Transported from air bases in Japan to McCord Air Force Base near Tacoma, Washington, the aluminum and other metals used in the chem trail spraying could be easily transported for use in Moses Lake, as U.S. Air Force and U.S. Navy planes regularly fly almost every day to and from McCord to Moses Lake. I have personally witnessed these same Orion P-130 U.S. Navy air craft taking off and landing at McCord Air Force Base.

In 2014, I had several tests done on the chemicals in the air, water, and fish of Moses Lake, Washington by the Wisconsin State Laboratory of Hygiene, after laboratories in the State of Washington refused to do any testing. The results of these tests included here.

(a)   OTW Wisconsin Lab Report_wslh_final 153979 47355 – Lake water in Moses Lake tested for various metals. Significant amounts of sulfur, aluminum, barium, and strontium were all found in the water. See attached lab report.

Sulfur	5100 ug/L
Aluminum	43.9 ug/L
Barium	31.0 ug/L
Strontium	172 ug/L

Wisconsin State Laboratory of Hygiene
2601 Agriculture Drive, PO Box 7996
Madison, WI 53707-7996
(800)442-4618 - FAX (608)224-6213
http://www.slh.wisc.edu

Laboratory Report

D.F. Kurtycz, M.D., Medical Director - Charles D. Brokopp, Dr.P.H., D

Environmental Health Division

DNR LAB ID: 113133790   NELAP LAB ID: E37658   EPA LAB ID: WI00007   WI DATCP ID: 105-415

WSLH Sample: 153979001

Report To:	Invoice To:
TED MAHR	TED MAHR

Customer ID: 346414

Collection Date: 8/25/2014 9:00:00 PM
Owner:

Unique Well #:   NA
Well Construction:
County:
Driller or Pump Installers License #:
Sampling Location: 5108 SHORECREST ROAD, N E
                     MOSES LAKE, WA 98837
Sampling Point: SWIMMING BEACH

Collected By: TED MAHR
Well Completion Date:

Date Received: 8/28/2014
Date Reported: 9/3/2014
Sample Reason: INVESTIGATION

Sample Comments

NON-SLH BOTTLE USED. RESULTS APPROXIMATE.

Metals, Total Recoverable

Analyte			Analysis Method	Result	Units	LOD	LOQ
Prep Date	09/02/14	Analysis Date 09/03/14					
Sulfur			E200.7 Metals, Trace Elements	5100	ug/L	20.0	60.0
Aluminum			E200.7 Metals, Trace Elements	43.9	ug/L	10.0	30.0
Barium			E200.7 Metals, Trace Elements	31.0	ug/L	1.00	3.00
Strontium			E200.7 Metals, Trace Elements	172	ug/L	1.00	3.00

Wisconsin State Laboratory of Hygiene
2601 Agriculture Drive, PO Box 7996
Madison, WI 53707-7996
(800)442-4618 - FAX (608)224-6213
http://www.slh.wisc.edu

Laboratory Report

D.F. Kurtycz, M.D., Medical Director - Charles D. Brokopp, Dr.P.H., D

Environmental Health Division

DNR LAB ID: 113133790   NELAP LAB ID: E37658   EPA LAB ID: WI00007   WI DATCP ID: 105-415

WSLH Sample: 153979001

The water microbiology unit analyzes samples as received and not all samples are tested for preservation before analysis is performed.

List of Abbreviations:
LOD = Level of detection
LOQ = Level of quantification
ND = None detected. Results are less than the LOD
* next to result = Result is between LOD and LOQ
^ next to result = Result is between 0 (zero) and LOD
LOD=LOQ, Limits were not statistically derived

Test results for NELAP accredited tests are certified to meet the requirements of the NELAC standards. For a list of accredited analytes
see http://www.slh.edu/nelap/

Responsible Party

Microbiology: Sharon Kluender, Lab Manager, 608-224-6262
Inorganic Chemistry: Tracy Hanke, Lab Manager, 608-224-6270
Metals: DeWayne Kennedy-Parker, Lab Manager, 608-224-6282
Organic Chemistry: David Webb, Lab Manager, 608-224-6200
Emergency Chemical Response: Noel Stanton, Lab Manager, 608-224-6251

Wisconsin State Laboratory of Hygiene
2601 Agriculture Drive, PO Box 7996
Madison, WI 53707-7996
(800)442-4618 - FAX (608)224-6213
http://www.slh.wisc.edu

Laboratory Report

D.F. Kurtycz, M.D., Medical Director - Charles D. Brokopp, Dr.P.H., Di...

Environmental Health Division

WDNR LAB ID: 113133790   NELAP LAB ID: E37658   EPA LAB ID: WI00007   WI DATCP ID: 105-415

WSLH Sample: 153979001

Drinking Water Standards for Result Interpretation

Parameter	Public Health Standard	Public Welfare Standard	Lifetime Health Advisory Limit
Aluminum	200 ug/L		
Arsenic (Total)	10 ug/L		
Atrazine*	3.0 ppb		
Cadmium	5 ug/L		
Calcium	No standard		
Chromium (Total)	100 ug/L		
Cobalt	40 ug/L		
Copper	1300 ug/L		
Fluoride	See below		
Hardness	No standard (see below)		
Iron		0.3 mg/L	
Lead	15 ug/L		
Magnesium	No standard		
Manganese	300 ug/L	50 ug/L	
Molybdenum			90 ug/L **
Nickel	100 ug/L		
Nitrate	10 mg/L		
Nitrate + Nitrite	10 mg/L		
Nitrite	1 mg/L		
Strontium			4000 ug/L (EPA)
Vanadium	30 ug/L		
Zinc		5000 ug/L	

Note: This table does not contain a complete list of standards. A complete list can be found in s. NR 140, Wis. Adm. Code.

Public Health Standard: Limit above which the water should not be consumed or used for food preparation. (s. NR 140.10, Wis. Adm. Code)

Public Welfare Standard: Limit above which the substance may adversely affect the cosmetic or aesthetic quality of drinking water. (s. NR 140.12, Wis. Adm. Code)

Lifetime Health Advisory Limit: Consuming water below this limit for a lifetime is not expected to cause adverse health effects. (United States Environmental Protection Agency (EPA) or Wisconsin Dept. of Health Services (WI DHS))

*The Atrazine standard includes Atrazine and its breakdown products.

**NR 140 currently lists a Public Health Standard for Molybdenum of 40 ug/L, however this number is based on the EPA Lifetime Health Advisory Limit which is currently under review. The 90 ug/L Lifetime Health Advisory is recommended by the WI Dept of Health Services and should be used in the evaluation of the safety of your drinking water.

Other analytes:	Concentration:	Interpretation:
Fluoride	0.7 mg/L	Optimal
	>2.0 mg/L	Children under 8 should not consume
	>4.0 mg/L	Children and adults should not consume
Hardness	<17.1 mg/L	Soft
	17.1-60 mg/L	Slightly hard
	60-120 mg/L	Moderately hard
	120-180 mg/L	Hard
	>180 mg/L	Very Hard

(b)   OTW Air Filter tests_wslh_final 156770 47355.pdf – Air tested for various metals with air filter. Hazardous and and extremely toxic levels of aluminum (7940 mg/kg), sodium (2440 mg/kg) and other metals were found. See attached lab report.

The level of aluminum, alone, makes it hazardous to even breathe the air in Moses Lake, Washington.   If Moses Lake, Washington was a work site covered by the U.S. Department of Labor OSHA regulations, the entire area would have to be immediately evacuated, according to Therese Aigner, an environmental consultant in Pennsylvania.

Wisconsin State Laboratory of Hygiene
2601 Agriculture Drive, PO Box 7996
Madison, WI 53707-7996
(800)442-4618 - FAX (608)224-6213
http://www.slh.wisc.edu

Laboratory Report

D.F. Kurtycz, M.D., Medical Director - Charles D. Brokopp, Dr.P.H.

Environmental Health Division

WDNR LAB ID: 113133790   NELAP LAB ID: E37658   EPA LAB ID: WI00007   WI DATCP ID: 105-415

WSLH Sample: 156770001

Report To:	Invoice To:
TED MAHR	TED MAHR

Customer ID: 346414

Field #:	CHARCOAL AIR FILTER	ID#:
Project No:		Sample Location:
Collection End:		Sample Description: CHARCOAL FILTER FROM KENMORE HEPA 200
Collection Start:		Sample Type:
Collected By: TED MAHR		Waterbody:
Date Received: 9/12/2014		Point or Outfall:
Date Reported: 9/24/2014		Sample Depth:
Sample Reason:		Program Code:
		Region Code:
		County:

Metals, Total

Analyte	Analysis Method	Result	Units	LOD	LOQ
Prep Date 09/16/14 Analysis Date 09/17/14					

Comments:

This sample was tested for twenty-six (26) metals using a qualitative technique. This technique is intended to be a screening tool to provide a general profile of the sample for a suite of metals and minerals. The concentration of these metals and minerals should be considered an approximation.

Analyte	Analysis Method	Result	Units	LOD	LOQ
Antimony	SW846 6010B	3.08	mg/kg	0.857	2.57
Arsenic	SW846 6010B	ND	mg/kg	0.857	2.57
Barium	SW846 6010B	32.4	mg/kg	0.428	1.37
Beryllium	SW846 6010B	0.152F	mg/kg	0.0857	0.257
Boron	SW846 6010B	23.9	mg/kg	1.71	5.14
Cadmium	SW846 6010B	0.343	mg/kg	0.0857	0.257
Calcium	SW846 6010B	2550	mg/kg	8.57	27.4
Chromium	SW846 6010B	17.3	mg/kg	0.428	1.37
Cobalt	SW846 6010B	3.94	mg/kg	0.428	1.37
Copper	SW846 6010B	50.2	mg/kg	0.428	1.37
Lead	SW846 6010B	2.06F	mg/kg	0.857	2.57
Magnesium	SW846 6010B	1550	mg/kg	8.57	27.4

Report ID: 1775714   Page 1 of 6   Report Rev 0000.25.2 WSL

| | Wisconsin State Laboratory of Hygiene
2601 Agriculture Drive, PO Box 7996
Madison, WI 53707-7996
(800)442-4618 - FAX (608)224-6213
http://www.slh.wisc.edu | **Laboratory Report** |

D.F. Kurtycz, M.D., Medical Director - Charles D. Brokopp, Dr.PH

Environmental Health Division

WDNR LAB ID: 113133790   NELAP LAB ID: E37658   EPA LAB ID: WI00007   WI DATCP ID: 105-4

WSLH Sample: 156770001

Metals, Total

Analyte		Analysis Method	Result	Units	LOD	LOQ
Prep Date	09/16/14	Analysis Date 09/17/14				
Manganese		SW846 6010B	114	mg/kg	0.428	1.37
Molybdenum		SW846 6010B	ND	mg/kg	0.857	2.57
Nickel		SW846 6010B	11.9	mg/kg	0.428	1.37
Selenium		SW846 6010B	ND	mg/kg	1.71	5.14
Silver		SW846 6010B	ND	mg/kg	0.857	2.57
Sodium		SW846 6010B	2440	mg/kg	8.57	27.4
Strontium		SW846 6010B	30.1	mg/kg	0.428	1.37
Thallium		SW846 6010B	2.48F	mg/kg	0.857	2.57
Vanadium		SW846 6010B	20.0	mg/kg	0.428	1.37
Zinc		SW846 6010B	31.5	mg/kg	0.428	1.37
Prep Date	09/18/14	Analysis Date 09/17/14				
Sulfur		SW846 6010B	1570	mg/kg	343	1030
Prep Date	09/16/14	Analysis Date 09/17/14				
Aluminum		SW846 6010B	7940	mg/kg	8.57	25.7
Iron		SW846 6010B	8260	mg/kg	85.7	274
Potassium		SW846 6010B	8810	mg/kg	85.7	274
Titanium		SW846 6010B	429	mg/kg	4.28	13.7

The water microbiology unit analyzes samples as received and not all samples are tested for preservation before analysis is performed.

List of Abbreviations:
LOD = Level of detection
LOQ = Level of quantification
ND = None detected. Results are less than the LOD
F next to result = Result is between LOD and LOQ
Z next to result = Result is between 0 (zero) and LOD
if LOD=LOQ, Limits were not statistically derived

*Test results for NELAP accredited tests are certified to meet the requirements of the NELAC standards. For a list of accredited analy
see http://www.slh.edu/nelap/

Report ID: 1775714   Page 2 of 6   Report Rev 0000.25.2.W

Wisconsin State Laboratory of Hygiene
2601 Agriculture Drive, PO Box 7996
Madison, WI 53707-7996
(800)442-4618 - FAX (608)224-6213
http://www.slh.wisc.edu

Laboratory Repor

D.F. Kurtycz, M.D., Medical Director - Charles D. Brokopp, D

Environmental Health Division

WDNR LAB ID: 113133790   NELAP LAB ID: E37658   EPA LAB ID: WI00007   WI DATCP ID: 10$

WSLH Sample: 156770001

Responsible Party

Microbiology: Sharon Kluender, Lab Manager, 608-224-6262
Inorganic Chemistry: Tracy Hanke, Lab Manager, 608-224-6270
Metals: DeWayne Kennedy-Parker, Lab Manager, 608-224-6282
Organic Chemistry: David Webb, Lab Manager, 608-224-6200
Emergency Chemical Response: Noel Stanton, Lab Manager, 608-224-6251

(c)   OTW – ML Water test results_wslh_final   160124 47355. PDF   --- Lake water in Moses Lake was tested for various metals.   Significant amounts of aluminum and strontium were found in the lake water.   See following report.

Wisconsin State Laboratory of Hygiene
2601 Agriculture Drive, PO Box 7996
Madison, WI 53707-7996
(800)442-4618 · FAX (608)224-6213
http://www.slh.wisc.edu

Laboratory Report

D.F. Kurtycz, M.D., Medical Director - Charles D. Brokopp, Dr.P.

Environmental Health Division

WDNR LAB ID: 113133790   NELAP LAB ID: E37658   EPA LAB ID: WI00007   WI DATCP ID: 105-4

WSLH Sample: 160124001

Report To: Invoice To:
TED MAHR   TED MAHR

Customer ID: 346414

Collection Date: 9/26/2014 10:00:00 AM   Collected By: TED MAHR
Owner: Well Completion Date:

Unique Well #: NA   Date Received: 9/29/2014
Well Construction: Date Reported: 10/2/2014
County: Sample Reason: INVESTIGATION
Driller or Pump Installers License #:
Sampling Location: 5108 SHORECREST ROAD, N.E.
                 MOSES LAKE, WA 98837
Sampling Point: OTHER

Sample Comments

NON-SLH BOTTLE USED. RESULTS APPROXIMATE.

SAMPLE SOURCE: LAKE WATER.

Metals, Total Recoverable

Analyte		Analysis Method	Result	Units	LOD	LOC
Prep Date 09/29/14	Analysis Date 10/01/14					
Aluminum		E200.7 Metals, Trace Elements	31.0	ug/L	10.0	30.0
Arsenic		E200.7 Metals, Trace Elements	ND	ug/L	5.00	16.0
Cadmium		E200.7 Metals, Trace Elements	ND	ug/L	1.00	3.00
Calcium		E200.7 Metals, Trace Elements	22.2	mg/L	0.100	0.30
Chromium		E200.7 Metals, Trace Elements	ND	ug/L	1.00	3.00
Cobalt		E200.7 Metals, Trace Elements	ND	ug/L	1.00	3.00
Copper		E200.7 Metals, Trace Elements	ND	ug/L	5.00	15.0
Iron		E200.7 Metals, Trace Elements	ND	mg/L	0.100	0.30

Wisconsin State Laboratory of Hygiene
2601 Agriculture Drive, PO Box 7996
Madison, WI 53707-7996
(800)442-4618 - FAX (608)224-6213
http://www.slh.wisc.edu

Laboratory Report

D.F. Kurtycz, M.D., Medical Director - Charles D. Brokopp, Dr.P.

Environmental Health Division

WDNR LAB ID: 113133790   NELAP LAB ID: E37658   EPA LAB ID: WI00007   WI DATCP ID: 105-4

WSLH Sample: 160124001

Metals, Total Recoverable

Analyte		Analysis Method	Result	Units	LOD	LOQ
Prep Date 09/29/14	Analysis Date 10/01/14					
Lead		E200.7 Metals, Trace Elements	ND	ug/L	3.00	10.0
Magnesium		E200.7 Metals, Trace Elements	12.6	mg/L	0.100	0.300
Manganese		E200.7 Metals, Trace Elements	5.00	ug/L	1.00	3.00
Nickel		E200.7 Metals, Trace Elements	ND	ug/L	2.00	6.00
Strontium		E200.7 Metals, Trace Elements	163	ug/L	1.00	3.00
Vanadium		E200.7 Metals, Trace Elements	11.0	ug/L	1.00	3.00
Zinc		E200.7 Metals, Trace Elements	ND	ug/L	5.00	15.0
Hardness (SM 2340B)		E200.7 Metals, Trace Elements	107	mg/L	1.40	4.60

The water microbiology unit analyzes samples as received and not all samples are tested for preservation before analysis is perform

List of Abbreviations:
LOD = Level of detection
LOQ = Level of quantification
ND = None detected. Results are less than the LOD
F next to result = Result is between LOD and LOQ
Z next to result = Result is between 0 (zero) and LOD
if LOD=LOQ, Limits were not statistically derived

*Test results for NELAP accredited tests are certified to meet the requirements of the NELAC standards. For a list of accredited analy
see http://www.slh.edu/nelap/

Previous Reports

This sample was previously reported under the following report ID(s): 1801260

Responsible Party

Microbiology: Sharon Kluender, Lab Manager, 608-224-6262
Inorganic Chemistry: Tracy Hanke, Lab Manager, 608-224-6270
Metals: DeWayne Kennedy-Parker, Lab Manager, 608-224-6282
Organic Chemistry: David Webb, Lab Manager, 608-224-6200
Emergency Chemical Response: Noel Stanton, Lab Manager, 608-224-6251

Wisconsin State Laboratory of Hygiene
2601 Agriculture Drive, PO Box 7996
Madison, WI 53707-7996
(800)442-4618 - FAX (608)224-6213
http://www.slh.wisc.edu

Laboratory Report

D.F. Kurtycz, M.D., Medical Director - Charles D. Brokopp, Dr.P.H

Environmental Health Division

WDNR LAB ID: 113133790   NELAP LAB ID: E37658   EPA LAB ID: WI00007   WI DATCP ID: 105-41

WSLH Sample: 160124001

Drinking Water Standards for Result Interpretation

Parameter	Public Health Standard	Public Welfare Standard	Lifetime Health Advisory Limit
Aluminum	200 ug/L		
Arsenic (Total)	10 ug/L		
Atrazine*	3.0 ppb		
Cadmium	5 ug/L		
Calcium	No standard		
Chromium (Total)	100 ug/L		
Cobalt	40 ug/L		
Copper	1300 ug/L		
Fluoride	See below		
Hardness	No standard (see below)		
Iron		0.3 mg/L	
Lead	15 ug/L		
Magnesium	No standard		
Manganese	300 ug/L	50 ug/L	
Molybdenum			90 ug/L **
Nickel	100 ug/L		
Nitrate	10 mg/L		
Nitrate + Nitrite	10 mg/L		
Nitrite	1 mg/L		
Strontium			4000 ug/L (EPA)
Vanadium	30 ug/L		
Zinc		5000 ug/L	

Note: This table does not contain a complete list of standards. A complete list can be found in s. NR 140, Wis. Adm. Code.

Public Health Standard: Limit above which the water should not be consumed or used for food
preparation. (s. NR 140.10, Wis. Adm. Code)

Public Welfare Standard: Limit above which the substance may adversely affect the cosmetic
or aesthetic quality of drinking water. (s. NR 140.12, Wis. Adm. Code)

Lifetime Health Advisory Limit: Consuming water below this limit for a lifetime is not expected to cause
adverse health effects. (United States Environmental Protection Agency (EPA) or Wisconsin Dept. of
Health Services (WI DHS))

*The Atrazine standard includes Atrazine and its breakdown products.

**NR 140 currently lists a Public Health Standard for Molybdenum of 40 ug/L, however this number is based on the EPA Lifetime Health Advisory Limit
is currently under review. The 90 ug/L Lifetime Health Advisory is recommended by the WI Dept of Health Services and should be used in the evaluati
the safety of your drinking water.

Other analytes:	Concentration:	Interpretation:
Fluoride	0.7 mg/L	Optimal
	>2.0 mg/L	Children under 8 should not consume
	>4.0 mg/L	Children and adults should not consume
Hardness	<17.1 mg/L	Soft
	17.1-60 mg/L	Slightly hard
	60-120 mg/L	Moderately hard
	120-180 mg/L	Hard
	>180 mg/L	Very Hard

Appendix D

Spiritual Protections
The Hu and White Light

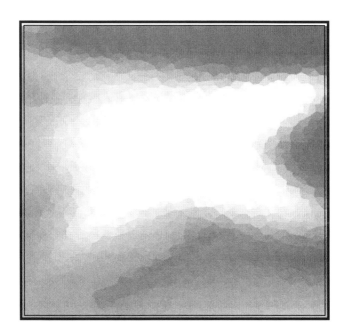

Each of us is a powerful, sovereign spiritual being, inhabiting a human body in order to evolve our consciousness. Self-protection is one of the most important lessons we can learn to spiritually advance. When confronted with a negative entity or situation, remember that the white light is always stronger than the dark and in a conflict between light and dark, or positive and negative, the positive light forces will always win!

Protecting yourself from negative people or situations is easy and can be done two ways: (a) with white light, and (b) by asking the Galactic Alliance for help. Furthermore, it is always a good idea to take the high road when dealing with a negative person or situation. Never lower yourself to the level of the antagonist. Energy flows where intention goes so by lowering yours vibrational level you simply add to an already negative situation Mahatma Gandhi expressed it best when he said, "always be the change you wish to see in the world."

To protect yourself with white light, visualize a cone of white light around you. Then around that light, visualize a series of mirrors facing outward which will reflect and deflect any negativity back to its source. Once this is done, ask the Supreme Being and the angels to keep this protection in place for a period of time say 12 to 24 hours and then thank them for their help.

In addition, you can also ask the Galactic Alliance for help and protection. To do this, chant the word "Hu" three to five times a day in a quiet place. If there are people around, and you want to keep this private chant the word silently to yourself. "Hu" comes from the word "human" and is very ancient. When you use this word as a meditation technique, it will open up your pineal gland and aid in the development of your psychic abilities and intuition. Using this as a meditation technique is a signal to the Galactics Alliance to assist you.

The "Galactic Alliance" is a shorter term for their formal name, which is: "The Galactic Alliance of Interdimensional Free Worlds." They consist of approximately 450 million planets, and 7 trillion entities, which are mostly (but not all) human. However, they are all benevolent; they all want to help us evolve. They are between 50,000 and 100,000 years ahead of us technologically, and between 30,000 and 50,000 years ahead of us technologically.

Using these two techniques will help protect you against any negativity, as well as guide you on your spiritual path. Please contact me anytime if you need help with these techniques. My email is: outofthisworld1150@gmail.com.

⌘   ⌘   ⌘

Made in the USA
Columbia, SC
08 September 2019